LONGMAN LITERATURE SHAKESPEARE

A Midsummer Night's Dream

William Shakespeare

Editors: Julia Markus and Paul Jordan

Longman Literature Shakespeare
Series editor: Roy Blatchford
Consultant: Jackie Head

Macbeth   0 582 08827 5
Romeo and Juliet   0 582 08836 4
The Merchant of Venice   0 582 08835 6
A Midsummer Night's Dream   0 582 08833 X
Twelfth Night   0 582 08834 8
Julius Caesar   0 582 08828 3

Other titles in the Longman Literature series are listed on page 245.

Contents

Introduction

Shakespeare's life and times

Shakespeare was born into a time of change. Important discoveries about the world were changing people's whole way of life, their thoughts and their beliefs. The fact that we know very little of Shakespeare's particular life story does not mean that we cannot step into his world.

What do we know about Shakespeare?

Imagine for a minute you are Shakespeare, born in 1564, the son of a businessman who is making his way in Stratford-upon-Avon. When you are thirteen, Francis Drake sets off on a dangerous sea voyage around the world, to prove that it is round, not flat, and to bring back riches. The trades people who pass in and out of your town bring with them stories of other countries, each with their own unique culture and language. You learn in school of ancient heroic myths taught through Latin and Greek, and often, to bring these stories alive, travelling theatres pass through the town acting, singing, performing, and bringing with them tales of London. But, at the age of fourteen your own world shifts a little under your feet; your father has got into serious debt, you find yourself having to grow up rather fast.

This is an unremarkable life so far – the death of your sisters is not an uncommon occurrence at this time, and even when you marry at eighteen, your bride already pregnant at the ceremony, you are not the first to live through life in this way. After your daughter, your wife gives birth to twins, a girl and a boy, one of whom dies when he is eleven. But before this, for some reason only you know, perhaps to do with some poaching you are involved in or because your marriage to a woman eight years older than you is having difficulties, you travel to London. There you eventually join the theatre, first as an actor and then as a writer. You write for the theatres in the inn yards, then for Queen Elizabeth in court, and when she dies, for King James I. As well as this you write for the large theatres which are being built in London: the Rose, the Globe, Blackfriars and the Swan. You die a rich man.

What did Shakespeare find in London?

When Shakespeare first travelled to London he found a city full of all that was best and worst in this new era of discovery. There was trade in expensive and fashionable items, a bubbling street life with street-theatre, pedlars of every sort, sellers of songs and poems. Industry was flourishing in textiles, mining, the manufacture of glass, iron, and sugar. The place to be known was the court of Queen Elizabeth. She was unmarried and drew many admirers even in her old age, maintaining a dazzling social world with her at its centre. There were writers and poets, grasping what they could of the new world, building on the literature of other countries, charting the lingering death of medieval life and the chaotic birth of something new.

By contrast, Shakespeare also found poverty, death and disease. The plague, spread by rats, found an easy home in these narrow streets, often spilling over with dirt and sewage: it killed 15,000 people in London in 1592 alone. It was an overcrowded city: the increased demand for wool for trade brought about the enclosure of land in the countryside, and this, coupled with bad harvests, brought the peasants, thrown off their land and made poor, into London to seek wealth.

What was England like in Shakespeare's day?

England was a proud nation. Elizabeth would not tolerate rivals and destroyed her enemies. In 1587 she had Mary Queen of Scots executed for treason, and in 1588 her navy defeated a huge armada of ships from Spain. Both acts were prompted by religion. In maintaining the Protestant Church of England her father, King Henry VIII, had established, Elizabeth stood out against a strong Catholic Europe. Within the Protestant religion too, there were divisions, producing extreme groups such as the Puritans who believed that much of the Elizabethan social scene was sinful, the theatres being one of their clearest targets for disapproval. Her power was threatened for other reasons too. In 1594 her doctor was executed for attempting to poison her, and in 1601 one of her favourites, the Earl of Essex, led an unsuccessful revolt against her.

When Elizabeth died in 1603 and James I succeeded her, he brought a change. He was a Scottish king, and traditionally Scotland and England had had an uneasy relationship. He was interested in witchcraft and he supported the arts, but not in the same way as Elizabeth had. He too met with treason, in the shape of Guy Fawkes and his followers, who in 1605 attempted to blow up The Houses of Parliament. If Shakespeare needed examples of life at its extremes, he had them all around him, and his closeness to the court meant he understood them more than most.

What other changes did Shakespeare see?

Towards the end of Shakespeare's life, in Italy, a man Shakespeare's age invented the telescope and looked at the stars. His radical discoveries caused him to be thrown out of the Catholic Church. For fifteen centuries people had believed in a picture of the universe as held in crystal spheres with order and beauty, and everything centring around the earth. In this belief the sun, moon and stars were the heavens; they ruled human fate, they were distant and magical. Galileo proved this was not so. So, the world was no longer flat and the earth was not the centre of the universe. It must have felt as if nothing was to be trusted anymore.

What do Shakespeare's plays show us about Elizabethan life?

Even without history books much of Shakespeare's life can be seen in his plays. They are written by one who knows of the tragedy of sudden death, and illness, and of the splendour of the life of the court in contrast to urban and rural poverty. He knows the ancient myths of the Greeks and Romans, the history of change in his own country, and, perhaps from reading the translations carried by merchants to London, he knows the literature of Spain and Italy.

His plays also contain all the hustle and bustle of normal life at the time. We see the court fool, the aristocracy, royalty, merchants and the servant classes. We hear of bear-baiting, fortune-telling, entertaining, drinking, dancing and singing. As new changes happen they are brought into the plays, in the form of maps, clocks, or the latest fashions. Shakespeare wrote to perform, and his plays were performed to bring financial reward. He studied his audience closely and produced what they wanted. Sometimes, as with the focus on witchcraft in *Macbeth* written for King James I, this was the celebration of something which fascinated them; sometimes, as with the character of Malvolio in *Twelfth Night*, it was the mockery of something they despised.

What do Shakespeare's plays tell us about life now?

You can read Shakespeare's plays to find out about Elizabethan life, but in them you will also see reflected back at you the unchanging aspects of humanity. It is as if in all that changed around him, Shakespeare looked for the things that would *not* change – like love, power, honour, friendship and loyalty – and put them to the test. In each he found strength and weakness.

We see *love*:
- at first sight,
- which is one-sided,
- between young lovers,
- in old age,
- between members of one family,
- lost and found again.

We see *power*:
- used and abused,
- in those who seek it,
- in those who protect it with loyalty,
- in the just and merciful rule of wise leaders,
- in the hands of wicked tyrants.

We see *honour*:
- in noble men and women,
- lost through foolishness,
- stolen away through trickery and disloyalty.

We see *friendship*:

- between men and men, women and women, men and women,
- between masters and servants,
- put to the test of jealousy, grief and misunderstanding.

These are just some examples of how Shakespeare explored in his plays what it was to be human. He lived for fifty-two years and wrote thirty-seven plays, as well as a great number of poems. Just in terms of output this is a remarkable achievement. What is even more remarkable is the way in which he provides a window for his audiences into all that is truly human, and it is this quality that often touches us today.

What are Comedies, Tragedies and Histories?

When Shakespeare died, his players brought together the works he had written, and had them published. Before this some of the plays had only really existed as actors' scripts written for their parts alone. Many plays in Shakespeare's day and before were not written down at all, but spoken, and kept in people's memories from generation to generation. So, making accurate copies of Shakespeare's plays was not easy and there is still some dispute over how close to the original scripts our current editions are. Ever since they were first published people have tried to make sense of them. Sometimes they are described under three headings: Comedy, Tragedy and History. The dates on the chart that follows refer to the dates of the first recorded performances or, if this is not known, the date of first publication. They may have been performed earlier but history has left us no record; dating the plays exactly is therefore difficult.

COMEDY	HISTORY	TRAGEDY
	King John (1590)	
	Henry VI, Part I (1592)	
Comedy of Errors (1594)		Titus Andronicus (1594)
The Taming of the Shrew (1594)		
Two Gentlemen of Verona (1594)		
The Merry Wives of Windsor (1597)	Richard II (1597)	Romeo and Juliet (1597)
	Richard III (1597)	
The Merchant of Venice (1598)	Henry IV, Part II (1598)	
Love's Labour's Lost (1598)		
As You Like It (1600)	Henry V (1600)	
A Midsummer Night's Dream (1600)	Henry VI, Part II (1600)	
Much Ado About Nothing (1600)	Henry VI, Part III (1600)	
Twelfth Night (1600)		
Troilus and Cressida (1601)		
		Hamlet (1602)
Measure for Measure (1604)	Henry IV, Part I (1604)	Othello (1604)
All's Well That Ends Well (1604)		

COMEDY	HISTORY	TRAGEDY
		Julius Caesar (1605)
		Macbeth (1606)
		King Lear (1606)
		Antony and Cleopatra (1608)
		Timon of Athens (1608)
		Coriolanus (1608)
Pericles (1609)		
Cymbeline (1611)		
The Winter's Tale (1611)		
The Tempest (1612)	*Henry VIII* (1612)	

Comedy = a play which maintains a thread of joy throughout and ends happily for most of its characters.

Tragedy = a play in which characters must struggle with circumstances and in which most meet death and despair.

History = a play focusing on a real event or series of events which actually happened in the past.

These three headings can be misleading. Many of the comedies have great sadness in them, and there is humour in most of the tragedies, some of which at least point to happier events in the future. Some of the tragedies, like *Macbeth* and *Julius Caesar*, make history their starting point.

We do not know exactly when each play was written but from what we know of when they were performed we can see that Shakespeare began by writing poetry, then histories and comedies. He wrote most of his tragedies in the last ten years of his life, and in his final writings wrote stories full of near-tragic problems which, by the end of the plays he resolved. Sometimes these final plays (*Pericles*, *Cymbeline*, *The Winter's Tale* and *The Tempest*) are called Comedies, sometimes they are called Romances or simply The Problem Plays.

Where were Shakespeare's plays performed?

Plays in Shakespeare's day were performed in several places, not just in specially designed theatres.

Inn Yard Theatre: Players performed in the open courtyard of Elizabethan inns. These were places where people could drink, eat and stay the night. They were popular places to make a break in a journey and to change or rest horses. Some inns built a permanent platform in the yard, and the audience could stand in the yard itself, or under shelter in the galleries which overlooked the yard. The audiences were lively and used to the active entertainment of bear-baiting, cock-fighting, wrestling and juggling. Plays performed here needed to be action-packed and appealing to a wide audience. In 1574 new regulations were made to control performances in response to the number of fights which regularly broke out in the audience.

Private House Theatre: The rich lords of Elizabethan times would pay travelling theatre companies to play in the large rooms of their own private houses for the benefit of their friends. There was no stage and the audience were all seated. Torches and candles were used to create artificial lighting. Costumes played an important part in creating atmosphere but there were no sets.

Public Hall Theatre: Some town councils would allow performances of plays in their grand halls and council buildings. As well as this, ceremonial halls such as the Queen's courts in Whitehall were frequently used in this way, as were halls at Hampton Court, Richmond and Greenwich Palace. For these performances, designed for a larger audience than those given in private houses, scaffolding would be arranged for tiered seating which would sur-round a central acting area. Audiences were limited to those with a high social standing.

Public Theatres: Unlike Public Hall theatres, these theatres were built for the purpose of presenting plays. At the end of the sixteenth century there were about 200,000 people living in London, and eleven public theatres showing performances. Of these, about half a dozen were so large that they seated about 2,000 people. The audiences, who were drawn from all sections of society, paid to see performances which began at 2 p.m. The audience sat in covered galleries around a circular acting area which was open air. Whilst the theatres stood within the City of London they were subject to its laws. They could not perform during times of worship, and they were closed during outbreaks of the plague. Theatres were often the scenes of fighting and because of the trouble this caused, in 1596 performances of plays were forbidden within the city boundaries. So people started building theatres outside the city on the south side of the River Thames.

What were the performances like?

To some extent this depended on the play being performed and the audience watching. A play performed before the court of the queen or king would need to be one that did not offend the ruler. Plays performed in the inn yard or the public theatres needed to have a wide appeal and several distractions such as dancing and music to keep the audience's attention.

Wherever they performed, the players had to create the illusion that the whole world could be seen inside their play. They had no sets, except in some cases tapestries which were hung up to show changes in scenery, but they did have bright costumes in which to perform. Scenes of battle or shipwreck were suggested by words rather than special effects, though we do know that they used burning torches, as it was due to a fire caused by one of these that the first Globe Theatre burnt down during a performance in 1613.

Actors joined together in companies, who would perform several different plays, and be sponsored by the nobility. Shakespeare became a key member of the Lord Chamberlain's company which Queen Elizabeth sponsored, and which went on to be called The King's Men when James I became king.

There were no women on the Elizabethan stage. Most female characters would be played by boys whose voices had not yet broken, or if it was an old character, by men in the company. Actors carried a reputation for being immoral and ungodly people, and were therefore thought unsuitable company for women. The men of Shakespeare's company became famous for playing particular types of characters such as the fool, the lover or the villain. Shakespeare probably created many of his parts with particular actors in mind.

Where can I find out more about Shakespeare?

Shakespeare is perhaps the world's most famous playwright and there is no shortage of books written about him. In your library or bookshop you will find books which look at:

- Shakespeare's life;
- the history of England under the reign of Queen Elizabeth I and James I;
- European history, art and literature of the sixteenth and seventeenth century;
- discoveries made throughout the world during Elizabethan times;
- characters, themes and ideas in Shakespeare's writing.

In Stratford-upon-Avon, where Shakespeare was born you can visit his birthplace, and much of the town consists of buildings which would have stood in Shakespeare's day. In addition to this there are many museums and exhibitions which tell more about Shakespeare's life and work.

Some theatrical companies today, such as the Royal Shakespeare Company, devote themselves to performing Shakespeare's plays in London, Stratford, and on tour around the country. They are always seeking new ways to bring the plays to life. However, perhaps the best way to find out more about Shakespeare is to study his plays by reading and acting them yourself and by seeing them in performance. Shakespeare wrote about what he knew, and the key to discovering how his mind and emotions worked is to look at what he wrote.

Shakespeare's language

Speaking Shakespeare

A Midsummer Night's Dream is a play, not a novel, so the lines were written to be heard by an audience in a theatre, not read silently to oneself. Speaking the lines can sound strange at first: it was written about four hundred years ago, and the English language has changed since then. Most of it is in verse, and of course no one goes around speaking verse naturally. The best way to start coming to terms with it is by practice.

Below are some extracts from the play to start you off. Remember:

- Pause at commas, colons and semi-colons.
- Take a breath at the full stops at the end of sentences.
- Don't pause at the end of lines unless the punctuation tells you to.
- Try to follow the meaning of the words, placing emphasis on appropriate words in order to get the meaning across.
- Read at normal speaking pace, not quicker or slower.
- Don't worry about making mistakes. Everyone does.

Colourful insults

When the four lovers are lost and bewitched in the wood, they fling around some richly colourful insults in their anger. With a partner, see if you can make these lines from Act 3, scene 2 sound really vicious!

HERMIA

Out, dog! Out, cur! (line 65)

LYSANDER

Hang off, thou cat, thou burr; vile thing, let loose,
Or I will shake thee from me like a serpent! (lines 260–1)

HERMIA

O me! you juggler, you canker-blossom,
You thief of love! What, have you come by night
And stolen my love's heart from him? (lines 282–4)

HERMIA

How low am I, thou painted maypole? Speak,
How low am I? I am not yet so low
But that my nails can reach unto thine eyes. (lines 296–8)

LYSANDER

Get you gone, you dwarf,
You minimus, of hindering knot-grass made,
You bead, you acorn. (lines 328–30)

An argument

When the workmen of Athens meet to plan their play, 'Pyramus and Thisby', their leader, Peter Quince, wants to give Flute the part of Thisby, the leading lady. Bottom, who has already been cast as Pyramus, wants the part too! Read this in a group of three.

QUINCE

Francis Flute, the bellos–mender.

FLUTE

Here, Peter Quince.

QUINCE

Flute, you must take Thisby on you.

FLUTE

What is Thisby, a wandering knight?

QUINCE

It is the lady that Pyramus must love.

FLUTE

Nay, faith, let not me play a woman; I have a beard coming.

QUINCE

That's all one; you shall play it in a mask, and you may speak as small as you will.

BOTTOM

An I may hide my face, let me play Thisby too: I'll speak in a monstrous little voice; 'Thisne, Thisne'. 'Ah Pyramus, my lover dear! thy Thisby dear, and lady dear!'

QUINCE

No, no, you must play Pyramus; and Flute, you Thisby.

BOTTOM

Well, proceed.

(Act 1, scene 2, lines 38–53)

Pictures in language

One of the distinctive things about *A Midsummer Night's Dream* is the number of times that characters paint pictures in words. Can you visualise them as you read them?

In the first example, Puck is describing a trick he plays on old women:

> The wisest aunt, telling the saddest tale,
> Sometime for three-foot stool mistaketh me;
> Then slip I from her bum, down topples she,
> And 'tailor' cries, and falls into a cough;
> And then the whole quire hold their hips, and laugh,
> And waxen in their mirth, and neeze, and swear
> A merrier hour was never wasted there.

(Act 2, scene 1, lines 51–7)

Here is Oberon describing the flowery bower where Titania sleeps:

> I know a bank whereon the wild thyme blows;
> Where oxlips and the nodding violet grows,
> Quite over-canopied with lucious woodbine,
> With sweet must-roses, and with eglantine;

(Act 2, scene 1, lines 249–52)

Finally, here is Oberon's colourful description of the dawn sun turning the sea to gold:

> I with the morning's love have oft made sport,
> And, like a forester, the groves may tread
> Even till the eastern gate, all fiery-red,
> Opening on Neptune, with fair blessed beams
> Turns into yellow gold his salt green streams.

(Act 3, scene 2, lines 389–93)

The language of love

Some people think that *A Midsummer Night's Dream* was written to celebrate a marriage. All the action concerns the ups and downs of love, and it ends with a triple marriage being celebrated with the performance of a play about tragic lovers. It is not surprising, then, that the language of love plays a large part in the play. However, the lovers in the play are often bewitched by

Oberon's love potion, which causes extreme and passionate infatuation. This is reflected in wild and exaggerated language. Shakespeare uses this opportunity to make us smile at the things people say under the influence of the madness of love. Try reading these extracts to a *close* friend!

To start with, here is a case of love at first sight. The bewitched Titania awakes to see the ass-headed Bottom:

> I pray thee, gentle mortal, sing again;
> Mine ear is much enamoured of thy note;
> So is mine eye enthralled to thy shape;
> And thy fair virtue's force perforce doth move me
> On the first view, to say, to swear love thee.

(Act 3, scene 1, lines 135–9)

Here is a second case of the same emotion. This time Demetrius wakes to see Helena:

> O Helen, goddess, nymph, perfect, divine,
> To what, my love, shall I compare thine eyne?
> Crystal is muddy: O how ripe in show
> Thy lips, those kissing cherries, tempting grow!

(Act 3, scene 2, lines 137–40)

Meanwhile, Bottom and Titania have been getting better acquainted! Here, Titania uses a beautiful simile comparing herself clinging to Bottom with the ivy clinging to the elm tree:

> … the female ivy so
> Enrings the barky fingers of the elm.
> O, how I love thee! how I dote on thee!

(Act 4, scene 1, lines 44–6)

Finally, in the workmens' play 'Pyramus and Thisby', the language of love is made fun by exaggeration. Here is the heart-broken Thisby comparing her dead lover to a variety of flowers, fruit and vegetables. Read this one with as much sincerity as you can:

> These lily lips,
> This cherry nose,
> These yellow cowslip cheeks,

Are gone, are gone:
Lovers, make moan:
His eyes were green as leeks.

(Act 5, scene 1, lines 320–5)

Prose and blank verse

Every Shakespearean play is written partly in *prose* (ordinary written language) and partly in *verse*, which may or may not rhyme. If it does not rhyme, it is called *blank verse*. For instance, in Act 1, scene 1 of *A Midsummer Night's Dream*, the first one hundred and seventy lines are in blank verse, and the rest of the scene is in rhyming *couplets* (pairs of lines which rhyme with one another). The three examples of 'pictures in language' on page xvii are all in rhyming couplets. In *A Midsummer Night's Dream*, Shakespeare uses more rhyme than he usually does; of his thirty-seven plays, only *Love's Labour's Lost* has more.

Most of the verse in the play has ten beats to a line. One of the most quoted lines in the play, 'The course of true love never did run smooth' (Act 1, scene 1, line 134), fits this pattern. Eight one-syllable words plus the two-syllable 'never' make up the ten beats.

Now look at a speech of Theseus's late in the play, where he is asking what entertainments are laid on for the evening of his wedding day. Try reading the lines out loud a few times with a partner, counting the number of beats in each line:

Come now, what masques, what dances shall we have 1
To wear away this long age of three hours 2
Between our after-supper, and bed-time? 3
Where is our usual manager of mirth? 4
What revels are in hand? Is there no play 5
To ease the anguish of a torturing hour? 6

(Act 5, scene 1, lines 32–7)

The first three lines of this extract are, in fact, one sentence, but each line begins with a capital letter. You can see from line 5 that sentences can end in the middle of lines, and from lines 1, 2 and 5 that there isn't necessarily punctuation at the end of lines. So when you are reading Shakespeare's verse, remember to follow the punctuation carefully.

Shakespeare sometimes shortens words to make them fit the beat. For instance, in Hippolyta's line: 'I love not to see wretchedness o'ercharged', (Act 5, scene 1, line 85) the last word has lost a syllable. Sometimes words ending in 'ed' have the last syllable sounded separately. In this edition, these are marked with an accent over the 'e'. For example, in these two lines of Titania's:

> By pavéd fountain, or by rushy brook,
> Or in the beachéd margent of the sea,

(Act 2, scene 1, lines 84–5)

'pavéd' and 'beachéd' are said as two-syllable words rather than one, making both lines conform to the regular ten-beat pattern.

Although ten-beat blank or rhymed verse makes up the bulk of the play, a variety of other forms of verse are used at times in *A Midsummer Night's Dream*, especially by the fairy characters. There are songs such as the fairies' lullaby to Titania in Act 2, scene 2. And Puck and Oberon sometimes use a seven-syllable line as in Puck's famous line 'Lord, what fools these mortals be!' (Act 3, scene 2, line 115)

The workmen of Bottom's amateur theatre group speak prose rather than verse, except in their play 'Pyramus and Thisby'. This conforms to Shakespeare's usual practice of giving prose to characters who are not of the nobility, such as servants and labourers. When Theseus speaks to Bottom in the last act, he too uses prose.

Images

You will have seen from the extracts you have read already that Shakespeare makes his words as full of meaning as possible. He often gets a character to tell a story that is so rich in ideas it is more like a painting. These pictures are formed by the use of *figurative* language such as *similes* and *metaphors*.

In the second speech of the play, Hippolyta uses a simile:

> And then the moon, like to a silver bow
> New bent in heaven, shall behold the night
> Of our solemnities.

(Act 1, scene 1, lines 9–11)

She compares the crescent moon to a bent bow made of silver. You can spot similes because they usually contain the words 'like' or 'as'. Can you find and explain the simile in Theseus's speech right at the beginning of the play?

A metaphor is also a comparison of two objects (like the moon and the bow above) but it does not contain the words 'like' or 'as'. In Act 1, Lysander is concerned that the woman he loves, Hermia, is looking pale:

> How now, my love? why is your cheek so pale?
> How chance the roses there do fade so fast?
>
> (Act 1, scene 1, lines 128–9)

He is comparing her pale cheeks to roses that have begun to fade. Hermia replies with a metaphor of her own. She says that the roses are fading because of lack of water, but that she could easily supply the water by crying, comparing her eyes to 'tempests':

> Belike for want of rain, which I could well
> Beteem them from the tempest of my eyes.
>
> (Act 1, scene 1, line 131)

Understanding the play

The practice extracts will have helped you to see how the language of the play is spoken. Speaking words correctly and looking out for figurative language will also help you to understand what the language means.

Here are some more ways to work out the meanings of words and phrases:

- **The words themselves**   Are they similar to modern words? Can you guess their meaning from this? Check the glossary for any that are new to you.

- **The context of the immediate lines**   Is there a general theme in the conversation or speech that might give you some clues?

- **The context of the scene**   Where and when is this scene taking place? What is the main action? Can you picture the scene and pick up clues from the setting?

- **The characters as you understand them**   When you saw this character before, was he or she funny, depressed, scared, serious? Can you guess at the sort of things this person might say and the sort of tone he or she is likely to adopt?

Don't worry if you don't understand every word. On your first reading, or hearing, what is important is getting the gist of what is being said. Shakespeare's language is rich in ideas and images. You do not have to understand it all at once: you can enjoy finding out more each time you revisit it.

The glossary: a word of warning

The glossary has been compiled to help you understand the language of the play. On occasions complex and beautiful poetry has been translated or paraphrased into mundane, straightforward prose. When this happens, some of the original meaning is bound to be lost. You are advised, therefore, to use the glossary as a help with your first reading, but once you feel you have the main gist of the meaning, you should try to rely on it less.

A Midsummer Night's Dream

CHARACTERS
in the play

THESEUS, *Duke of Athens*

EGEUS, *father of Hermia*

LYSANDER
DEMETRIUS } *in love with Hermia*

PHILOSTRATE, *provider of the Duke's entertainments*

QUINCE, *a carpenter*

SNUG, *a joiner*

BOTTOM, *a weaver*

FLUTE, *a bellows-mender*

SNOUT, *a tinker*

STARVELING, *a tailor*

HIPPOLYTA, *Queen of the Amazons, a nation of women fighters, betrothed to Theseus*

HERMIA, *daughter of Egeus, in love with Lysander*

HELENA, *in love with Demetrius*

OBERON, *King of the Fairies*

TITANIA, *Queen of the Fairies*

PUCK, *or* ROBIN GOODFELLOW, *a spirit of mischief*

PEASEBLOSSOM
COBWEB
MOTH } *fairies*
MUSTARDSEED

The scenes are in Athens and a wood near it.

3

David Gooderson as Quince: the New Shakespeare Company at the Open Air
Theatre, Regent's Park, 1991 (photograph © Alastair Muir).

Act 1: summary

Theseus, Duke of Athens, and Hippolyta, former Queen of the Amazons, are planning to marry in four days' time. This will mark the end of the war between their states. Theseus orders plays, music and dancing to be prepared for the wedding celebrations.

Egeus, a noble Athenian, complains to Theseus about his daughter Hermia. He wants her to marry Demetrius but she has refused because she is in love with Lysander. Hermia asks what will happen to her if she carries on defying her father. Theseus tells her that according to the law of Athens, unless she marries Demetrius as Egeus wishes, she must choose between death or life in a convent – for ever away from the company of men. Lysander complains that Demetrius was planning to marry Helena, a friend of Hermia's, but has since deserted her.

After the others have left, Hermia and Lysander make plans to run away together to a place beyond the reach of the law of Athens, and to marry secretly. They arrange to meet in the wood outside the town. They tell Helena of their plans and she in turn decides to tell their secret to Demetrius in an attempt to win back his favour.

News of the Duke's wedding has reached a group of amateur actors, led by Peter Quince, a carpenter. They decide to put on a play about Pyramus and Thisby, two lovers who in Greek myth were forbidden to meet by their parents. Their star actor, Nick Bottom, a weaver, wants to play several parts but has to be satisfied with taking the leading man's role, Pyramus. They decide to rehearse secretly at night in the wood outside Athens.

1 *our nuptial hour*   time set for our wedding.

2 *Draws on apace*   approaches fast.

2–3 *four ... moon*   in four days' time there will be a new moon.

4 *she lingers my desires*   she makes me wait for what I want.

5 *step-dame, or a dowager*   step-mother or father's widow.

6 *Long ... revenue*   making a young man wait for a long time to inherit his dead father's property.

7 *steep*   soak.

11 *solemnities*   wedding ceremony.

12 *Athenian youth*   young people of Athens.

13 *pert and nimble*   lively and agile.

14 *Turn ... funerals*   reserve sad feelings for funerals.

15 *the pale ... pomp*   melancholy is not appropriate at our festivities.

16–17 *I wooed thee ... injuries*   the wedding marks the end of the war between Athens, led by Duke Theseus, and the Amazons, whose Queen was Hippolyta.

Act One

Scene one

Athens.

Enter THESEUS, HIPPOLYTA, PHILOSTRATE, *and* ATTENDANTS.

Happiness

THESEUS

    Now, fair Hippolyta, our nuptial hour
    Draws on apace: four happy days bring in
    Another moon: but O, methinks how slow
    This old moon wanes; she lingers my desires
    Like to a step-dame, or a dowager,   5
    Long withering out a young man's revenue.

HIPPOLYTA

    Four days will quickly steep themselves in night;
    Four nights will quickly dream away the time;
    And then the moon, like to a silver bow
    New bent in heaven, shall behold the night   10
    Of our solemnities.

THESEUS

              Go, Philostrate,
    Stir up the Athenian youth to merriments;
    Awake the pert and nimble spirit of mirth;
    Turn melancholy forth to funerals:
    The pale companion is not for our pomp.   15

                      Exit PHILOSTRATE

    Hippolyta, I wooed thee with my sword,
    And won thy love doing thee injuries;

18 *another key*   in a different style; this is a reference to a musical change of key.

19 *revelling*   celebrating; high-spirited behaviour.

22 *vexation*   frustration and anger.

27 *bewitched ... my child*   made my daughter fall in love with him. Egeus thinks Lysander has cast a spell on Hermia.

28 *rhymes*   love poems.

31 *With feigning voice ... feigning love*   with a voice that is pretending to be sincere, songs about an insincere love.

32 *stolen ... her fantasy*   captured her imagination.

34–5 *messengers ... unhardened youth*   tokens which are extremely persuasive to innocent young people.

36 *filched*   stolen.

39 *Be it so*   if.

41 *ancient privilege*   long-established right.

But I will wed thee in another key,
With pomp, with triumph, and with revelling.

Enter EGEUS *and his daughter* HERMIA, LYSANDER, *and*
DEMETRIUS.

EGEUS

Happy be Theseus, our renownéd Duke!   20

THESEUS

Thanks, good Egeus: what's the news with thee?

EGEUS *brings shadow*

Full of vexation come I, with complaint
Against my child, my daughter Hermia.
Stand forth, Demetrius. My noble lord,
This man hath my consent to marry her.   25
Stand forth, Lysander; and, my gracious Duke,
This man hath bewitched the bosom of my child:
Thou, thou Lysander, thou hast given her rhymes,
And interchanged love-tokens with my child:
Thou hast by moonlight at her window sung,   30
With feigning voice, verses of feigning love,
And stolen the impression of her fantasy
With bracelets of thy hair, rings, gawds, conceits,
Knacks, trifles, nosegays, sweetmeats, messengers
Of strong prevailment in unhardened youth;   35
With cunning hast thou filched my daughter's
    heart,
Turned her obedience, which is due to me,
To stubborn harshness. And, my gracious Duke,
Be it so she will not here before your Grace
Consent to marry with Demetrius,   40
I beg the ancient privilege of Athens;
As she is mine, I may dispose of her;
Which shall be either to this gentleman,

9

48–51 *One that ... him imprinted* Theseus reminds Hermia that she takes after her
father in appearance, like a wax model.

51 *figure* model.

disfigure destroy; note the poetic use of the two similar words.

54 *in this kind* in a matter such as this.

wanting ... voice without your father's permission.

56 *would* wish.

60 *concern my modesty* affect my reputation for quietness and decency.

61 *In such a presence* such company (i.e. the Duke).

plead my thoughts express my opinions.

63 *befall* happen to.

65 *abjure* give up.

society company.

Or to her death, according to our law
Immediately provided in that case.   45

THESEUS
What say you, Hermia? be advised, fair maid.
To you your father should be as a god;
One that composed your beauties; yea, and one
To whom you are but as a form in wax
By him imprinted; and within his power   50
To leave the figure, or disfigure it.
Demetrius is a worthy gentleman.

HERMIA
So is Lysander.

THESEUS
            In himself he is;
But in this kind, wanting your father's voice,
The other must be held the worthier.   55

HERMIA
I would my father looked but with my eyes.

THESEUS
Rather your eyes must with his judgement look.

HERMIA
I do entreat your Grace to pardon me.
I know not by what power I am made bold,
Nor how it may concern my modesty   60
In such a presence here to plead my thoughts;
But I beseech your Grace, that I may know
The worst that may befall me in this case,
If I refuse to wed Demetrius.

THESUS
Either to die the death, or to abjure   65
For ever the society of men.

11

67 *question your desires* think carefully about what you want.

68 *Know of your youth ... blood* remember that you are young and look carefully at yourself.

70 *endure the livery of a nun* put up with the clothing, and so the life of, a nun.

71 *aye* ever.

  mewed enclosed.

73 *fruitless moon* reference to Diana the goddess of the moon and also of virginity.

74 *master so their blood* are able to control their passions.

75 *maiden pilgrimage* life of chastity.

76–8 *But earthlier ... single blessedness* but on earth, the rose which is picked and used for perfume (distilled) is happier than that which is left to wither on the bush. The idea is that a married life is pleasanter than a single one for a woman, however blessed or holy this might be.

80 *virgin patent* right to remain a virgin.

81 *his lordship* reference to Demetrius.

  unwishéd yoke unwanted domination. A yoke is the heavy wooden frame used to link two oxen together for pulling a plough; thus a symbol of submission and in this case marriage.

82 *sovereignty* power to rule.

84 *sealing-day* day on which the wedding contract is sealed; wedding day.

88 *would* wishes, wants.

89 *Diana's altar* Diana, goddess of the moon and of virginity, referred to in line 73 above.

  protest vow.

90 *For aye* for ever.

  austerity harshly simple way of life.

92 *crazéd title* flawed, invalid claim.

94 *do you marry him* Lysander sarcastically suggests that Demetrius should go and marry Egeus and leave him Hermia.

12

Therefore, fair Hermia, question your desires,
Know of your youth, examine well your blood.
Whether, if you yield not your father's choice,
You can endure the livery of a nun,   70
For aye to be in shady cloister mewed,
To live a barren sister all your life,
Chanting faint hymns to the cold fruitless moon.
Thrice blessèd they that master so their blood
To undergo such maiden pilgrimage;   75
But earthlier happy is the rose distilled
Than that which, withering on the virgin thorn,
Grows, lives, and dies in single blessedness.

HERMIA

So will I grow, so live, so die, my lord,
Ere I will yield my virgin patent up   80
Unto his lordship, whose unwishèd yoke,
My soul consents not to give sovereignty.

THESEUS

Take time to pause, and by the next new moon,
The sealing-day betwixt my love and me
For everlasting bond of fellowship,   85
Upon that day either prepare to die
For disobedience to your father's will,
Or else to wed Demetrius as he would,
Or on Diana's altar to protest
For aye austerity and single life.   90

DEMETRIUS

Relent, sweet Hermia, and Lysander, yield
Thy crazèd title to my certain right.

LYSANDER

You have her father's love, Demetrius:
Let me have Hermia's; do you marry him.

13

96 *render*   give to.

98 *estate*   hand over.

99 *well derived*   of as noble a family.

100 *well possessed*   rich.

101 *fortunes ... fairly ranked*   prospects in life considered to be as good.

102 *with vantage*   even better.

104 *of*   by.

105 *prosecute my right*   carry on making my claim.

106 *avouch it to his head*   say it to his face.

107 *Made love to*   let her know he loved her.

108 *won her soul*   had his love returned.

109 *dotes in idolatry*   worships him like a god.

110 *spotted*   dishonourable.
  inconstant   unfaithful, changeable.

113 *over-full of self-affairs*   too tied up with my own business.

114 *My mind did lose it*   I forgot it.

116 *private schooling*   confidential advice.

117–18 *look you ... father's will*   be prepared to go along with what your father wishes.

120 *extenuate*   lessen, make easier.

122 *what cheer*   how are you?

14

EGEUS

Scornful Lysander, true, he hath my love;   95
And what is mine my love shall render him;
And she is mine, and all my right of her
I do estate unto Demetrius.

LYSANDER

I am, my Lord, as well derived as he,
As well possessed; my love is more than his;   100
My fortunes every way as fairly ranked,
If not with vantage, as Demetrius';
And, which is more than all these boasts can be,
I am beloved of beauteous Hermia.
Why should not I then prosecute my right?   105
Demetrius, I'll avouch it to his head,
Made love to Nedar's daughter, Helena,
And won her soul: and she, sweet lady, dotes,
Devoutly dotes, dotes in idolatry,
Upon this spotted and inconstant man.   110

THESEUS

I must confess that I have heard so much,
And with Demetrius thought to have spoke thereof:
But being over-full of self-affairs,
My mind did lose it. But Demetrius, come,
And come Egeus, you shall go with me;   115
I have some private schooling for you both.
For you, fair Hermia, look you arm yourself
To fit your fancies to your father's will;
Or else the law of Athens yields you up –
Which by no means we may extenuate –   120
To death, or to a vow of single life.
Come, my Hippolyta; what cheer, my love?
Demetrius and Egeus, go along:
I must employ you in some business

125 *Against our nuptial*   in preparation for our wedding.

126 *nearly*   closely.

129 *How chance*   why do.

130 *Belike*   probably.

131 *beteem*   soak.

tempest of my eyes   Hermia's sad predicament is causing her to shed floods of tears.

132 *Ay me*   Lysander is sighing.

for aught   from anything.

135 *different in blood*   unsuitable because the couple came from different social classes.

136 *O cross! too high to be enthralled to low*   what a troublesome burden! to be too nobly born to be bound to someone of lower birth.

137 *misgraffèd in respect of years*   mismatched in their ages.

139 *stood upon the choice of friends*   depended on the choice of guardians or relatives.

141 *sympathy in choice*   perfect match.

Against our nuptial, and confer with you   125
Of something nearly that concerns yourselves.

EGEUS

With duty and desire we follow you.

Exeunt. LYSANDER *and* HERMIA *remain*

LYSANDER

How now, my love? why is your cheek so pale?
How chance the roses there do fade so fast?

HERMIA

Belike for want of rain, which I could well   130
Beteem them from the tempest of my eyes.

LYSANDER

Ay me; for aught that I could ever read,
Could ever hear by tale or history,
The course of true love never did run smooth;
But either it was different in blood –   135

HERMIA

O cross! too high to be enthralled to low.

LYSANDER

Or else misgraffed, in respect of years. –

HERMIA

O spite! too old to be engaged to young.

LYSANDER

Or else it stood upon the choice of friends –

HERMIA

O hell! to choose love by another's eyes.   140

LYSANDER

Or, if there were a sympathy in choice,

142   *lay seige to it*   threaten to destroy it.

145   *collied*   darkened.

146   *spleen*   sudden flash of anger; organ in the stomach once thought to be the seat of anger.

   unfolds   reveals.

147   *ere*   before.

150   *ever crossed*   always frustrated.

151   *edict in destiny*   law of fate.

152   *teach our trial patience*   learn to be patient about our misfortune.

153   *customary cross*   usual and expected burden.

155   *fancy's followers*   things that occur as a result of love.

156   *A good persuasion*   that's good advice.

157–8   *a dowager...revenue*   widow with a large income.

159   *remote seven leagues*   about twenty miles away.

160   *respects*   treats.

162–3   *the sharp... pursue us*   the harsh law of Athens has no power over us.

164   *Steal forth*   secretly escape from.

165   *without*   outside.

167   *To do...May*   to carry out the ceremonies of May Day.

168   *stay*   wait.

169   *Cupid's strongest bow*   Cupid was the classical god of love, usually shown holding a bow and arrows. Being shot by an arrow from Cupid's bow symbolised falling in love.

War, death, or sickness did lay siege to it;
Making it momentary as a sound,
Swift as a shadow, short as any dream,
Brief as the lightning in the collied night, 145
That in a spleen unfolds both heaven and earth,
And ere a man hath power to say, Behold!
The jaws of darkness do devour it up;
So quick bright things come to confusion.

HERMIA

If then true lovers have been ever crossed, 150
It stands as an edict in destiny.
Then let us teach our trial patience,
Because it is a customary cross,
As due to love as thoughts, and dreams, and sighs,
Wishes and tears, poor fancy's followers. 155

LYSANDER

A good persuasion; therefore hear me, Hermia:
I have a widow aunt, a dowager
Of great revenue, and she hath no child;
From Athens is her house remote seven leagues,
And she respects me as her only son. 160
There, gentle Hermia, may I marry thee;
And to that place the sharp Athenian law
Cannot pursue us. If thou lov'st me, then,
Steal forth thy father's house tomorrow night;
And in the wood, a league without the town, 165
Where I did meet thee once with Helena
To do observance to a morn of May,
There will I stay for thee.

HERMIA

                      My good Lysander,
I swear to thee by Cupid's strongest bow,

171 *simplicity* innocence.

Venus' doves Venus was the classical goddess of love, the mother of Cupid. She was often pictured with doves.

172 *knitteth* unites.

prospers helps love to blossom.

173–4 *And by ... was seen* reference to the fire on which Dido, Queen of Carthage, burned herself when Aeneas ('the false Troyan') deserted her by sailing away; from Vergil's poem *The Aeneid*.

180 *whither away?* where are you going?

181 *That fair again unsay* take back the word 'fair'.

182 *fair* beauty.

183 *lode-stars* stars used by sailors for navigation, believed by people in Shakespeare's day to have magnetic power.

tongue's sweet air voice's sweet sound.

184 *tuneable* pleasantly tuneful.

186–7 *sickness is catching ... fair Hermia* Helena wishes she could 'catch' some of Hermia's beauty – 'favour' – as one catches an illness.

190 *bated* excepted.

191 *to you translated* turned into you.

192 *with what art ... heart!* how skilfully you control Demetrius' emotions.

By his best arrow with the golden head,   170
By the simplicity of Venus' doves,
By that which knitteth souls and prospers loves,
And by that fire which burned the Carthage
    Queen
When the false Troyan under sail was seen,
By all the vows that ever men have broke,   175
In number more than ever women spoke,
In that same place thou hast appointed me,
Tomorrow truly will I meet with thee.

LYSANDER
Keep promise, love. Look, here comes Helena.

Enter HELENA.

HERMIA
God speed, fair Helena, whither away?   180

HELENA
Call you me fair? That fair again unsay.
Demetrius loves your fair. O happy fair!
Your eyes are lode-stars, and your tongue's sweet
    air
More tuneable than lark to shepherd's ear,
When wheat is green, when hawthorn buds
    appear.   185
Sickness is catching; O, were favour so,
Yours would I catch, fair Hermia, ere I go.
My ear should catch your voice, my eye your eye,
My tongue should catch your tongue's sweet
    melody.
Were the world mine, Demetrius being bated,   190
The rest I'll give to be to you translated.
O teach me how you look and with what art
You sway the motion of Demetrius' heart!

200 *His folly ... mine* it isn't my fault that he's so foolish. Hermia is assuring Helena that she is not trying to make Demetrius love her, in fact quite the opposite. Helena wishes she had such an effect on him.

201 *would* I wish.

203 *fly* escape from.

206 *graces* qualities.

208 *our minds we will unfold* we will let you into our secret.

209 *Phoebe* another name for Diana, goddess of the moon.

210 *visage* face.

watery glass mirror made by a smooth stretch of water.

211 *Decking ... liquid pearl* decorating with dew drops, which in Shakespeare's time were thought to fall from the moon.

HERMIA

I frown upon him, yet he loves me still.

HELENA

O that your frowns would teach my smiles such
    skill!   195

HERMIA

I give him curses, yet he gives me love.

HELENA

O that my prayers could such affection move!

HERMIA

The more I hate, the more he follows me.

HELENA

The more I love, the more he hateth me.

HERMIA

His folly, Helena, is no fault of mine.   200

HELENA

None but your beauty; would that fault were mine!

HERMIA

Take comfort: he no more shall see my face;
Lysander and myself will fly this place.
Before the time I did Lysander see,
Seemed Athens as a paradise to me.   205
O then, what graces in my love do dwell,
That he hath turned a heaven unto a hell!

LYSANDER

Helen, to you our minds we will unfold.
Tomorrow night, when Phoebe doth behold
Her silver visage in the watery glass,   210
Decking with liquid pearl the bladed grass,

212 *still*   always.

213 *devised to steal*   planned to escape.

215 *faint*   pale. Primroses are pale yellow spring flowers.

   wont   in the habit of doing something.

216 *Emptying ... counsel sweet*   telling each other our closest secrets.

219 *stranger companies*   company of people whom we do not know.

222 *Keep word*   keep your promise.

222–3 *we must ... lovers' food*   we must deprive ourselves of the sight of one another.

224 *adieu*   goodbye.

225 *As you ... on you*   we hope that Demetrius comes to love you as much as you love him.

226 *How happy ... can be*   how much happier some people can be than others!

229 *He will ... do know*   he will not acknowledge what everyone except him knows.

230 *errs*   is led astray.

232 *holding no quantity*   having no real value.

233 *transpose*   transform.

234 *Love looks ... mind*   people in love see what they want to see, rather than what is really there.

235 *Cupid painted blind*   pictures of Cupid often show him wearing a blindfold.

236 *Nor hath ... taste*   someone in love is unable to make proper judgements.

237 *figure*   represent.

   unheedy   careless.

239 *beguiled*   deceived.

A time that lovers' flights doth still conceal,
Through Athens' gates have we devised to steal.

HERMIA

And in the wood, where often you and I
Upon faint primrose-beds were wont to lie,   215
Emptying our bosoms of their counsel sweet,
There, my Lysander and myself shall meet,
And thence from Athens turn away our eyes
To seek new friends and stranger companies.
Farewell, sweet playfellow; pray thou for us;   220
And good luck grant thee thy Demetrius.
Keep word, Lysander; we must starve our sight
From lovers' food, till morrow deep midnight.

LYSANDER

I will, my Hermia. (*Exit* HERMIA) Helena, adieu.
As you on him, Demetrius dote on you!   225

                                        Exit LYSANDER

HELENA

How happy some o'er other some can be!
Through Athens I am thought as fair as she.
But what of that? Demetrius thinks not so;
He will not know what all but he do know:
And as he errs, doting on Hermia's eyes,   230
So I, admiring of his qualities.
Things base and vile, holding no quantity,
Love can transpose to form and dignity.
Love looks not with the eyes, but with the mind,
And therefore is winged Cupid painted blind.   235
Nor hath Love's mind of any judgement taste;
Wings, and no eyes, figure unheedy haste;
And therefore is Love said to be a child,
Because in choice he is so oft beguiled.

25

240 *waggish*   cheeky.

themselves forswear   fail to keep their word.

241 *the boy Love ... everywhere*   the boy Love – Cupid – is cheated everywhere; the implication is that people often treat love lightly and are not sincere when they say they are in love.

242 *ere*   until.

eyne   eyes.

248 *intelligence*   information.

249 *If I have thanks ... expense*   if Demetrius thanks me it will be (i) precious to me and (ii) dearly-bought (because I have betrayed Hermia to get it).

250 *herein ... my pain*   this way I mean to get some compensation for having suffered.

251 *To have ... back again*   by proving to Demetrius that she told him the truth about Hermia's plans, Helena hopes to win back his love.

2 *You were best*   you had better.

generally   Bottom often uses words he doesn't understand in his efforts to appear important and clever. 'Generally' means all at once, the opposite of 'man by man'. He ought to have used a word such as individually.

3 *according to the scrip*   as they are listed in the script which Quince has with him.

5 *fit*   able.

play   perform.

6 *interlude*   play.

As waggish boys in game themselves forswear; 240
So the boy Love is perjured everywhere;
For ere Demetrius looked on Hermia's eyne,
He hailed down oaths that he was only mine;
And when this hail some heat from Hermia felt,
So he dissolved, and showers of oaths did melt. 245
I will go tell him of fair Hermia's flight;
Then to the wood will he tomorrow night
Pursue her; and for this intelligence,
If I have thanks, it is a dear expense.
But herein mean I to enrich my pain, 250
To have his sight thither, and back again.

Exit

Scene two

Athens.

Enter QUINCE *the carpenter,* SNUG *the joiner,* BOTTOM *the weaver,* FLUTE *the bellows-mender,* SNOUT *the tinker, and* STAR-VELING *the tailor.*

QUINCE

Is all our company here?

BOTTOM

You were best to call them generally, man by man, according to the scrip.

QUINCE

Here is the scroll of every man's name, which is thought fit, through all Athens, to play in our 5
interlude before the Duke and the Duchess on his wedding-day at night.

27

8–9 *treats on*   deals with.

9–10 *grow to a point*   come to a conclusion.

11 *Marry*   by the Virgin Mary; a mild swear word, meaning something like O.K.

12 *Pyramus and Thisby*   two lovers in a Greek myth whose parents did not approve of their relationship.

21 *ask*   need.

22 *look to their eyes*   be prepared to be moved to tears.

23 *condole in some measure*   express my grief quite strongly.

24 *my chief humour ... tyrant*   I am best at playing the part of a tyrant.

25 *Ercles*   Hercules, a mythical Greek hero of enormous strength and courage.

rarely   extremely well.

25–6 *a part to tear ... all split*   part demanding lots of roaring and swaggering, with lots of violence.

27–34 *The raging ... foolish Fates*   Bottom gives an example of the sort of language he feels he is best at using on stage. (Shakespeare is mocking the rather bad verse used in popular plays of the time.)

BOTTOM

First, good Peter Quince, say what the play treats
on: then read the names of the actors: and so grow
to a point.   10

QUINCE

Marry, our play is: 'The most lamentable comedy
and most cruel death of Pyramus and Thisby'.

BOTTOM

A very good piece of work, I assure you, and a
merry. Now, good Peter Quince, call forth your
actors by the scroll. Masters, spread yourselves.   15

QUINCE

Answer as I call you. Nick Bottom, the weaver.

BOTTOM

Ready; name what part I am for, and proceed.

QUINCE

You, Nick Bottom, are set down for Pyramus.

BOTTOM

What is Pyramus, a lover or a tyrant?

QUINCE

A lover, that kills himself most gallant for love.   20

BOTTOM

That will ask some tears in the true performing of
it. If I do it, let the audience look to their eyes: I
will move storms; I will condole in some measure.
To the rest – yet my chief humour is for a tyrant.
I could play Ercles rarely, or a part to tear a cat 25
in, to make all split:
The raging rocks
And shivering shocks

31 *Phoebus' car* in Greek mythology, the sun was pulled across the sky in the chariot of the sun-god.

34 *Fates* in Greek mythology, the Fates were three sisters who controlled the destiny of all men and women.

36 *Ercles' vein* the style suitable for a hero; see page 28, note to line 25.

37 *condoling* intimate and sympathetic.

43 *faith* exclamation meaning by my faith.

45 *That's all one* that doesn't matter.

46 *small* quiet and high-pitched, like a woman's voice.

47 *An* if.

48–50 *'Thisne ... lady dear'* Bottom demonstrates his 'little voice'. He speaks first as Pyramus, then replies as Thisby.

Shall break the locks
Of prison-gates;   30
And Phoebus' car
Shall shine from far,
And make and mar
The foolish Fates.
This was lofty! Now name the rest of the players. 35
This is Ercles' vein, a tyrant's vein: a lover is more
condoling.

QUINCE
Francis Flute, the bellows-mender.

FLUTE
Here, Peter Quince.

QUINCE
Flute, you must take Thisby on you.   40

FLUTE
What is Thisby, a wandering knight?

QUINCE
It is the lady that Pyramus must love.

FLUTE
Nay, faith, let not me play a woman; I have a
beard coming.

QUINCE
That's all one; you shall play it in a mask, and 45
you may speak as small as you will.

BOTTOM
An I may hide my face, let me play Thisby too:
I'll speak in a monstrous little voice: 'Thisne,
Thisne'. 'Ah Pyramus, my lover dear! thy Thisby
dear, and lady dear!'   50

31

61 *fitted*   fully and suitably cast.
63 *slow of study*   slow at learning lines.
64 *extempore*   without a script, roaring whenever it is suitable.

QUINCE

No, no, you must play Pyramus; and Flute, you
Thisby.

BOTTOM

Well, proceed.

QUINCE

Robin Starveling, the tailor.

STARVELING

Here, Peter Quince.   55

QUINCE

Robin Starveling, you must play Thisby's mother.
Tom Snout, the tinker.

SNOUT

Here, Peter Quince.

QUINCE

You, Pyramus' father; myself, Thisby's father;
Snug the joiner, you, the lion's part: and I hope, 60
here is a play fitted.

SNUG

Have you the lion's part written? Pray you, if it be,
give it me, for I am slow of study.

QUINCE

You may do it extempore, for it is nothing but
roaring.   65

BOTTOM

Let me play the lion too; I will roar that I will do
any man's heart good to hear me. I will roar, that
I will make the Duke say, 'Let him roar again, let
him roar again.'

70 *An*   if.

terribly   terrifyingly.

fright   frighten.

76 *aggravate*   make worse – but Bottom means the opposite to this.

77–8 *sucking dove*   Bottom is confusing sucking lambs with sitting doves, two proverbially gentle beasts.

78 *roar you an 't were*   roar for you as if it were.

80 *sweet-faced*   handsome.

proper   manly; Quince is desperately trying to persuade Bottom to take the part.

82 *must needs*   must of necessity; Quince is flattering Bottom by saying no one else is fit for the part.

86 *discharge*   perform.

88 *French-crown-coloured*   gold, the colour of a French coin.

90 *Some of ... at all*   some French men are completely bald, with bare 'crowns' (heads). Quince is making a joke about the baldness caused by syphilis, commonly known in Shakespeare's day as French disease.

QUINCE

An you should do it too terribly, you would fright 70
the Duchess and the ladies, that they would shriek;
and that were enough to hang us all.

ALL

That would hang us, every mother's son.

BOTTOM

I grant you, friends, if you should fright the ladies
out of their wits, they would have no more discre- 75
tion but to hang us; but I will aggravate my voice
so, that I will roar you as gently as any sucking
dove; I will roar you an 't were any nightingale.

QUINCE

You can play no part but Pyramus; for Pyramus
is a sweet-faced man, a proper man as one shall see 80
in a summer's day, a most lovely, gentleman-like-
man; therefore you must needs play Pyramus.

BOTTOM

Well, I will undertake it. What beard were I best
to play it in?

QUINCE

Why, what you will. 85

BOTTOM

I will discharge it, in either your straw-colour
beard, your orange-tawny beard, your purple-in-
grain beard, or your French-crown-coloured beard,
your perfect yellow.

QUINCE

Some of your French crowns have no hair at all, 90
and then you will play bare-faced. But, masters,

92 *I am to*   I must.

93 *con*   learn; get to know.

95 *without*   outside.

97 *dogged*   pestered.

devices   plans.

98 *bill of properties*   list of articles – or props – needed for staging the play.

101 *obscenely*   Bottom uses the wrong word again. He clearly does not mean offensively or disgustingly!

take pains   make a big effort.

101–2 *be perfect*   know your lines perfectly.

104 *hold or cut bow-strings*   the precise meaning of this is not clear, but the sense seems to be keep to your word or be disgraced.

here are your parts, and I am to entreat you,
request you, and desire you, to con them by
tomorrow night; and meet me in the palace wood,
a mile without the town, by moonlight. There will 95
we rehearse: for if we meet in the city, we shall be
dogged with company, and our devices known. In
the mean time I will draw a bill of properties, such
as our play wants. I pray you, fail me not.

BOTTOM

We will meet, and there we may rehearse most 100
obscenely and courageously. Take pains; be
perfect; adieu.

QUINCE

At the Duke's oak we meet.

BOTTOM

Enough; hold or cut bow-strings.

Exeunt

Simon Deacon as Demetrius and Sandra James Young as Helena: London Bubble Theatre, 1988 (photograph: Steve Hickey).

Act 2: summary

In the wood outside Athens, we meet Puck, a mischievous spirit who serves Oberon, King of the Fairies. Puck is telling a fairy of an argument between Oberon and his Queen, Titania, over a little Indian boy whom they both want as an attendant. Titania has refused to give him up to her husband.

Oberon and Titania meet. Titania accuses Oberon of being in love with Hippolyta, while Oberon retaliates by accusing Titania of loving Theseus. Titania says that since their quarrel began, the weather and the seasons have been thrown into turmoil. Titania still refuses to give up the Indian boy.

After she has swept off, Oberon plans vengeance. He tells Puck to go and fetch a magic flower. If the juice of this flower is put onto the eyes of someone sleeping, they will fall in love with the first thing they see when they wake up.

Oberon is interrupted by Demetrius, who has followed Helena's advice to come to the wood to find Hermia before Lysander can marry her. Helena has followed him. Oberon, having made himself invisible, witnesses Demetrius' cruel treatment of the love-sick Helena. When Puck returns with the magic flower, Oberon takes some of the juice to use on Titania's eyes. Puck is ordered to take the rest and find Demetrius to smear his eyes too while he is asleep, so that he will fall in love with Helena on waking. Oberon creeps up on Titania as she sleeps, and successfully carries out his plan.

Lysander and Hermia have got lost in their efforts to get through the woods. They decide to sleep on the ground until morning. Puck comes upon them and mistakes Lysander for Demetrius: Oberon had simply told him to look for a young man in Athenian clothes. Puck drops the juice on Lysander's eyes and leaves. Demetrius runs in, still trying to escape from Helena. She cannot keep up, and finds Lysander lying on the ground. She wakes him up, and under the influence of the magic flower, he instantly falls in love with her. Helena is amazed, and assumes Lysander is just pretending to love her to make fun of her. She runs off, and Lysander runs after her. Hermia then wakes in the middle of a nightmare, to find herself alone and deserted.

3 *Thorough* through.

4 *pale* fence.

9 *dew her orbs upon the green* sprinkle her fairy rings ('orbs') with dew. Fairy rings are circles of darker grass on lawns or meadows ('the green') caused by the outer edge of an underground toadstool or mushroom patch. They were believed to be formed by fairies dancing.

10 *cowslips* yellow wild flowers which bloom in the late spring. At 10–15cm, they are not 'tall' except to a little fairy.

pensioners soldiers in the personal bodyguard of Queen Elizabeth I. They were selected for their height.

11–12 *In their gold ... rubies* Cowslips have red spots, likened here to rubies.

12 *favours* gifts.

13 *savours* scents.

16 *Lob* name given to a country buffoon or bumpkin.

17 *anon* soon.

20 *passing fell and wrath* very fierce and angry.

Act Two

Scene one

A wood near Athens.

Enter a Fairy at one side, and PUCK *at another.*

PUCK

  How now, spirit, whither wander you?

FAIRY

  Over hill, over dale,
  Thorough bush, thorough brier,
  Over park, over pale,
  Thorough flood, thorough fire;   5
  I do wander everywhere,
  Swifter than the moonés sphere;
  And I serve the Fairy Queen,
  To dew her orbs upon the green.
  The cowslips tall her pensioners be;   10
  In their gold coats spots you see,
  Those be rubies, fairy favours,
  In those freckles live their savours.
  I must go seek some dew-drops here,
  And hang a pearl in every cowslip's ear.   15
  Farewell, thou Lob of spirits; I'll be gone;
  Our Queen and all her elves come here anon.

PUCK

  The King doth keep his revels here tonight;
  Take heed the Queen come not within his sight;
  For Oberon is passing fell and wrath,   20
  Because that she as her attendant hath
  A lovely boy stolen from an Indian King;

23 *changeling*   child who was swapped for another at birth.
25 *Knight of his train*   one of the knights who attend him.
   trace   range through.
26 *perforce*   by force.
28 *they*   Oberon and Titania.
29 *sheen*   shining.
30 *square*   face each other in anger, as in 'square up'.
31 *them*   themselves.
32 *your shape and making quite*   your build completely.
33 *knavish*   mischievous.
34 *sprite*   spirit.
35 *villagery*   villagers.
36 *quern*   churn, the container in which butter is made from milk.
37 *bootless*   uselessly, pointlessly.
38 *barm*   froth, which ought to form the 'head' of beer.
44 *jest*   make jokes to, act as jester to.
45 *beguile*   charm, fascinate.
46 *filly foal*   young female horse.
47 *gossip*   woman who is too talkative.
48 *In very likeness of*   looking just like.
   crab   small apple that was roasted and put into beer to warm it up.
50 *dewlap*   folds of skin around her throat.

She never had so sweet a changeling.
And jealous Oberon would have the child
Knight of his train, to trace the forests wild;   25
But she perforce withholds the lovéd boy,
Crowns him with flowers, and makes him all her
   joy.
And now they never meet in grove or green,
By fountain clear, or spangled starlight sheen,
But they do square, that all their elves for fear   30
Creep into acorn cups and hide them there.

FAIRY

Either I mistake your shape and making quite,
Or else you are that shrewd and knavish sprite
Called Robin Goodfellow. Are not you he,
That frights the maidens of the villagery,   35
Skim milk, and sometimes labour in the quern,
And bootless make the breathless housewife churn,
And sometimes make the drink to bear no barm,
Mislead night-wanderers, laughing at their harm?
Those that Hobgoblin call you, and sweet Puck,   40
You do their work, and they shall have good luck.
Are not you he?

PUCK

         Thou speak'st aright;
I am that merry wanderer of the night.
I jest to Oberon, and make him smile,
When I a fat and bean-fed horse beguile,   45
Neighing in likeness of a filly foal;
And sometimes lurk I in gossip's bowl,
In very likeness of a roasted crab;
And when she drinks, against her lips I bob,
And on her withered dewlap pour the ale.   50

43

52 *three-foot*   three-legged.

54 *tailor*   exclamation meaning Oh! my tail (or bum!).

     falls into a cough   starts a coughing fit.

55 *quire*   people present.

56 *waxen*   increase.

     neeze   sneeze.

57 *room*   make room.

     train   (stage direction) followers and attendants.

60 *Ill met*   how unfortunate to have met you.

61 *Fairies, skip hence*   Fairies, come away.

62 *forsworn*   vowed to give up.

63 *Tarry*   wait.

     rash wanton   hasty, wilful creature.

     lord   husband and so – he would like to think! – her master.

66 *Corin*   name for a love-sick shepherd in classical stories.

67 *pipes of corn*   musical pipes made from straw stalks.

     versing love   singing love songs.

68 *Phillida*   traditional name for Corin's loved one in classical stories. See also note
to line 66 above.

69 *steep*   hills.

70 *forsooth*   truly.

     the bounding Amazon   she is referring sarcastically to Hippolyta, queen of the
Amazons, who she says Oberon is in love with.

71 *buskined*   wearing high hunting boots.

44

The wisest aunt, telling the saddest tale,
Sometime for three-foot stool mistaketh me;
Then slip I from her bum, down topples she,
And 'tailor' cries, and falls into a cough;
And then the whole quire hold their hips, and
    laugh,   55
And waxen in their mirth, and neeze, and swear
A merrier hour was never wasted there.
But room, fairy! here comes Oberon.

FAIRY

And here my mistress! Would that he were gone!

Enter OBERON *King of the Fairies at one side with his train,
and* TITANIA *the Queen at another with hers.*

OBERON

Ill met by moonlight, proud Titania.   60

TITANIA

What, jealous Oberon? Fairies, skip hence:
I have forsworn his bed and company.

OBERON

Tarry, rash wanton; am not I thy lord?
TITANIA

Then I must be thy lady; but I know
When thou hast stolen away from fairy land,   65
And in the shape of Corin sat all day,
Playing on pipes of corn, and versing love
To amorous Phillida. Why art thou here,
Come from the farthest steep of India,
But that, forsooth, the bouncing Amazon,   70
Your buskined mistress, and your warrior love,
To Theseus must be wedded; and you come
To give their bed joy and prosperity.

75 *Glance at*   make rude remarks about; take a swipe at.

credit   reputation.

78–80 *Peregenia ... Aegles ... Ariadne ... Antiopa*   various women with whom Theseus has been in love in the past.

81 *forgeries*   lies.

82 *middle summer's spring*   beginning of the midsummer season.

83 *we*   Titania and her fairies.

84 *pavéd fountain*   clear fountain with a pebbly bottom.

rushy   with rushes at the sides.

85 *margent*   border.

86 *ringlets*   dances in a fairy ring.

87 *brawls*   ruffian-like behaviour.

90 *Contagious*   disease-bearing.

91 *pelting*   minor.

92 *overborne their continents*   overflowed their banks.

93 *yoke*   harness.

94 *lost his sweat*   wasted his efforts.

94–5 *green corn ... a beard*   green (unripe) corn has rotted before it has developed the bristly, beard-like head that it has when mature.

96 *drownéd*   flooded.

97 *fatted with*   made fat by.

murrion flock   dead, diseased sheep.

98–100 *nine men's morris ... undistinguishable*   nine men's morris was an outdoor summer game, played on paths ('quaint mazes') cut out from the turf of a field ('green'). Now the bad weather has caused the paths to clog with mud and become overgrown.

101 *want*   lack.

winter cheer   because wintery weather is occurring out of season, people are deprived of the festivities (i.e. Christmas) that usually cheer them up.

103 *governess of floods*   controller of the tides.

OBERON

How canst thou thus, for shame, Titania,
Glance at my credit with Hippolyta,   75
Knowing I know thy love to Theseus?
Didst thou not lead him through the glimmering
   night
From Peregenia, whom he ravishéd?
And make him with fair Aegles break his faith,
With Ariadne, and Antiopa?   80

TITANIA

These are the forgeries of jealousy;
And never since the middle summer's spring
Met we on hill, in dale, forest, or mead,
By pavéd fountain, or by rushy brook,
Or in the beachéd margent of the sea,   85
To dance our ringlets to the whistling wind,
But with thy brawls thou hast disturbed our sport.
Therefore the winds, piping to us in vain,
As in revenge have sucked up from the sea
Contagious fogs; which, falling in the land,   90
Have every pelting river made so proud
That they have overborne their continents.
The ox hath therefore stretched his yoke in vain,
The ploughman lost his sweat, and the green corn
Hath rotted ere his youth attained a beard: 95
The fold stands empty in the drownéd field,
And crows are fatted with the murrion flock;
The nine men's morris is filled up with mud,
And the quaint mazes in the wanton green,
For lack of tread, are undistinguishable.   100
The human mortals want their winter cheer;
No night is now with hymn or carol blest;
Therefore the moon, the governess of floods,

47

104 *washes*   makes moist.

105 *rheumatic diseases*   colds and flu as well as rheumatism.

106 *thorough*   through.

   distemperature   upset in the weather.

107 *hoary-headed*   covered with greyish-white hairs, like an old man. The frost makes everything white.

109 *Hiem's ... crown*   winter's head.

110 *odorous chaplet*   sweet-smelling garland or wreath.

112 *childing*   fruitful (as in child-bearing).

113 *wonted liveries*   usual clothing.

   mazéd   amazed.

114 *increase*   what they bring forth. (Summer is producing frosts, and winter flowers.)

115 *progeny*   offspring.

116 *debate*   argument.

   dissension   disagreement.

117 *original*   source.

118 *Do you amend it*   it is up to you to put it right.

   it lies in you   it is your responsibility.

119 *cross*   upset.

120 *but*   only.

121 *henchman*   page.

122 *The fairy ... of me*   I would not exchange him for all your domain.

123 *votaress*   woman who has taken a religious vow to worship Titania.

126 *Neptune*   god of the sea.

127 *Marking th' embarkéd traders on the flood*   watching the ships used for trade sailing on the floodtide.

128 *conceive*   swell with wind, looking like pregnant women.

130 *swimming gait*   walking as though gliding through water.

48

Pale in her anger, washes all the air,
That rheumatic diseases do abound.   105
And thorough this distemperature we see
The seasons alter; hoary-headed frosts
Fall in the fresh lap of the crimson rose,
And on old Hiem's thin and icy crown
An odorous chaplet of sweet summer buds   110
Is, as in mockery, set. The spring, the summer,
The childing autumn, angry winter, change
Their wonted liveries, and the mazéd world,
By their increase, now knows not which is which.
And this same progeny of evils comes   115
From our debate, from our dissension;
We are their parents and original.

OBERON

Do you amend it, then; it lies in you.
Why should Titania cross her Oberon?
I do but beg a little changeling boy   120
To be my henchman.

TITANIA

            Set your heart at rest;
The fairy land buys not the child of me.
His mother was a votaress of my order,
And in the spicéd Indian air, by night,
Full often hath she gossiped by my side;   125
And sat with me on Neptune's yellow sands,
Marking th' embarkéd traders on the flood;
When we have laughed to see the sails conceive,
And grow big-bellied with the wanton wind;
Which she with pretty and with swimming gait   130
Following, her womb then rich with my young
    squire,
Would imitate, and sail upon the land

135 *of that boy did die*   died as a result of giving birth to the boy.

138 *intend you stay*   do you intend to stay.

139 *Perchance*   perhaps.

140 *round*   fairy circle.

142 *spare your haunts*   stay away from the places you usually go.

145 *chide downright*   surely quarrel.

146 *not from*   not go from.

149 *Since once*   the time when.

 promontory   headland jutting into the sea.

151 *dulcet and harmonious breath*   sweet and tuneful singing.

152 *rude*   rough.

 civil   calm.

153 *spheres*   places in the heavens.

To fetch me trifles; and return again,
As from a voyage, rich with merchandise.
But she, being mortal, of that boy did die;   135
And for her sake do I rear up her boy,
And for her sake I will not part with him.

OBERON

How long within this wood intend you stay?

TITANIA

Perchance till after Theseus' wedding-day.
If you will patiently dance in our round,   140
And see our moonlight revels, go with us;
If not, shun me, and I will spare your haunts.

OBERON

Give me that boy, and I will go with thee.

TITANIA

Not for thy fairy kingdom. Fairies, away:
We shall chide downright, if I longer stay.   145

Exit TITANIA *with her train*

OBERON

Well, go thy way; thou shalt not from this grove,
Till I torment thee for this injury.
My gentle Puck, come hither. Thou rememb'rest
Since once I sat upon a promontory,
And heard a mermaid on a dolphin's back   150
Uttering such dulcet and harmonious breath
That the rude sea grew civil at her song,
And certain stars shot madly from their spheres
To hear the sea-maid's music.

PUCK

                                    I remember.

157   *Cupid, all armed*   the god of love armed with his bow and arrow.

      certain   sure, accurate.

158   *fair vestal*   beautiful virgin.

159   *loosed his love-shaft*   shot his arrow.

161   *might*   could.

162   *Quenched in ... moon*   the arrow was put out by moonbeams, and so failed to reach its target. Diana, the goddess of the moon, was also the goddess of chastity, and protector of threatened virgins.

163   *imperial*   royal. This, together with 'thronéd' (line 158) is circumstantial evidence that the 'vestal' referred to is Queen Elizabeth I, the Virgin Queen, who ruled England while Shakespeare was alive.

      vot'ress   woman who has taken vows, in this case of chastity.

164   *fancy-free*   free of love.

165   *marked*   noted.

165   *bolt*   arrow.

166–8   *It fell ... Love-in-idleness*   the arrow fell on what we now call a pansy, which is often purple with white streaks.

171   *or man or woman*   either man or woman.

      madly dote   adore insanely.

174   *Ere*   before.

      leviathan   a huge sea monster.

      league   about three miles.

175   *put a girdle round about*   encircle.

181   *busy*   prying, as in busybody.

OBERON

That very time I saw, but thou couldst not,   155
Flying between the cold moon and the earth,
Cupid, all armed; a certain aim he took
At a fair vestal thronéd by the west,
And loosed his love-shaft smartly from his bow
As it should pierce a hundred thousand hearts;   160
But I might see young Cupid's fiery shaft
Quenched in the chaste beams of the watery moon;
And the imperial vot'ress passéd on,
In maiden meditation, fancy-free.
Yet marked I where the bolt of Cupid fell: 165
It fell upon a little western flower;
Before, milk-white, now purple with love's wound,
And maidens call it Love-in-idleness.
Fetch me that flower, the herb I shewed thee once.
The juice of it on sleeping eye-lids laid   170
Will make or man or woman madly dote
Upon the next live creature that it sees.
Fetch me this herb, and be thou here again
Ere the leviathan can swim a league.

PUCK

I'll put a girdle round about the earth   175
In forty minutes.

Exit PUCK

OBERON

                    Having once this juice,
I'll watch Titania when she is asleep,
And drop the liquor of it in her eyes:
The next thing then she waking looks upon,
Be it on lion, bear, or wolf, or bull,   180
On meddling monkey, or on busy ape,

53

183 *ere*   before.

185 *render up*   hand over.

186 *I am invisible*   the human characters about to enter are unable to see Oberon.

187 *conference*   conversation.

190 *The one ... slayeth me*   I want to kill Lysander, but Hermia is killing me because she will not love me.

191 *were stolen*   had crept stealthily.

192 *and wood*   and mad.

195 *adamant*   magnet and very hard stone.

196 *draw*   attract.

197 *Leave you*   if you will abandon.

199 *speak you fair*   say pleasant things to you.

203 *spaniel*   faithful dog, with a reputation for loving its owner however badly it is treated.

204 *fawn*   cringe and flatter.

205 *spurn*   kick.

She shall pursue it with the soul of love.
And ere I take this charm from off her sight,
As I can take it with another herb,
I'll make her render up her page to me.   185
But who comes here? I am invisible,
And I will overhear their conference.

Enter DEMETRIUS, HELENA *following him.*

DEMETRIUS

I love thee not, therefore pursue me not.
Where is Lysander, and fair Hermia?
The one I'll slay, the other slayeth me.   190
Thou told'st me they were stolen unto this wood;
And here am I, and wood within this wood,
Because I cannot meet my Hermia.
Hence, get thee gone, and follow me no more!

HELENA

You draw me, you hard-hearted adamant,   195
But yet you draw not iron, for my heart
Is true as steel. Leave you your power to draw,
And I shall have no power to follow you.

DEMETRIUS

Do I entice you? Do I speak you fair?
Or rather do I not in plainest truth   200
Tell you I do not nor I cannot love you?

HELENA

And even for that do I love you the more.
I am your spaniel; and, Demetrius,
The more you beat me, I will fawn on you.
Use me but as your spaniel; spurn me, strike me, 205
Neglect me, lose me; only give me leave,
Unworthy as I am, to follow you.

211 *Tempt not ... spirit*   don't push me too far.

214 *impeach your modesty*   put your reputation at risk. Demetrius is also suggesting that she is putting herself physically at risk as well.

215 *commit*   hand over, trust.

217–19 *To trust ... virginity*   to put your precious virginity at risk at night in a lonely and deserted place.

220 *privilege*   protection.

     for that   because.

223 *worlds of company*   a great number of people.

227 *brakes*   bushes.

230 *the story shall be changed*   the usual story (man chases woman) will be reversed.

231 *Apollo ... Daphne*   in the classical myth Apollo loved and chased after Daphne.

232 *griffin*   mythical beast, with an eagle's head and wings and a lion's body.

     hind   female deer.

What worser place can I beg in your love,
And yet a place of high respect with me,
Than to be uséd as you use your dog?   210

DEMETRIUS

Tempt not too much the hatred of my spirit;
For I am sick when I do look on thee.

HELENA

And I am sick when I look not on you.

DEMETRIUS

You do impeach your modesty too much,
To leave the city and commit yourself   215
Into the hands of one that loves you not;
To trust the opportunity of night
And the ill counsel of a desert place
With the rich worth of your virginity.

HELENA

Your virtue is my privilege: for that   220
It is not night when I do see your face,
Therefore I think I am not in the night;
Nor doth this wood lack worlds of company,
For you, in my respect, are all the world.
Then how can it be said I am alone,   225
When all the world is here to look on me?

DEMETRIUS

I'll run from thee and hide me in the brakes,
And leave thee to the mercy of wild beasts.

HELENA

The wildest hath not such a heart as you.
Run when you will, the story shall be changed: 230
Apollo flies, and Daphne holds the chase;
The dove pursues the griffin, the mild hind

gendue reversal embarrassment

233 *bootless*   useless.

235 *stay*   wait for.

239 *Fie*   (exclamation) shame on you!

240 *Your wrongs ... my sex*   your mistreatment of me makes me act in a way that is frowned upon in a woman – i.e. to chase after a man.

245 *nymph*   girl; Oberon means Helena.

246 *fly him*   run away from him.

247 *the flower*   the magical Love-in-idleness described by Oberon. See page 52, note to lines 166–8.

249–52 *thyme ... eglantine*   Oberon lists a variety of beautiful and fragrant wild flowers and herbs.

249 *blows*   blooms.

Makes speed to catch the tiger; bootless speed,
When cowardice pursues, and valour flies.

DEMETRIUS

I will not stay thy questions; let me go;   235
Or, if thou follow me, do not believe
But I shall do thee mischief in the wood.

HELENA

Ay, in the temple, in the town, the field
You do me mischief. Fie, Demetrius;
Your wrongs do set a scandal on my sex: 240
We cannot fight for love, as men may do;
We should be wooed, and were not made to woo.

Exit DEMETRIUS

I'll follow thee, and make a heaven of hell,
To die upon the hand I love so well.

Exit HELENA

OBERON

Fare thee well, nymph; ere he do leave this grove, 245
Thou shalt fly him, and he shall seek thy love.

Re-enter PUCK.

Hast thou the flower there? Welcome, wanderer.

PUCK

Ay, there it is.

OBERON

I pray thee give it me.
I know a bank whereon the wild thyme blows;
Where oxlips and the nodding violet grows,   250
Quite over-canopied with luscious woodbine,
With sweet musk-roses, and with eglantine;

253 *sometime of* at some period during.

254 *lulled* soothed to sleep.

255 *throws* sheds – snakes cast off their skin each year.

enamelled smooth and colourful, like enamel.

256 *Weed* clothing.

261 *disdainful* one who despises another.

262 *espies* sees.

265 *Effect it* do it.

266 *fond on* in love with.

267 *look thou* see that you.

ere the first cock crow cocks crow at dawn, when fairies are supposed to leave the world of humans.

1 *roundel* dance in a circle.

3 *cankers* plant diseases.

4 *rere-mice* bats, whose leathery wings are used to make fairy coats.

6 *clamorous* noisy.

There sleeps Titania sometime of the night,
Lulled in those flowers with dances and delight;
And there the snake throws her enamelled skin,   255
Weed wide enough to wrap a fairy in;
And with the juice of this I'll streak her eyes,
And make her full of hateful fantasies.
Take thou some of it, and seek through this grove:
A sweet Athenian lady is in love   260
With a disdainful youth: anoint his eyes;
But do it when the next thing he espies
May be the lady. Thou shalt know the man
By the Athenian garments he hath on.
Effect it with some care, that he may prove   265
More fond on her than she upon her love;
And look thou meet me ere the first cock crow.

PUCK
Fear not, my lord; your servant shall do so.

Exeunt

Scene two

The wood, with TITANIA'S *sleeping-place behind.*

Enter TITANIA, *with her train.*

TITANIA
Come now, a roundel, and a fairy song;
Then, for the third part of a minute, hence;
Some to kill cankers in the musk-rose buds.
Some war with rere-mice for their leathern wings,
To make my small elves coats, and some keep back 5
The clamorous owl that nightly hoots and wonders

7 *quaint* dainty.

8 *offices* duties.

9 *double* forked.

11 *blind-worms* slow-worms (which are in fact not poisonous).

13 *Philomel* classical name for the nightingale.

17 *nigh* near.

25 *aloof stand sentinel* keep guard at a distance.

At our quaint spirits. Sing me now asleep;
Then to your offices, and let me rest.

The fairies sing.

FIRST FAIRY

> *You spotted snakes with double tongue,*
> *Thorny hedgehogs, be not seen;*   10
> *Newts and blind-worms, do no wrong;*
> *Come not near our Fairy Queen.*

CHORUS

> *Philomel with melody*
> *Sing in our sweet lullaby;*
> *Lulla, lulla, lullaby, lulla, lulla, lullaby.*   15
> *Never harm, nor spell, nor charm,*
> *Come our lovely Lady nigh.*
> *So good night, with lullaby.*

SECOND FAIRY

> *Weaving spiders, come not here,*
> *Hence, you long-legg'd spinners, hence;*   20
> *Beetles black, approach not near;*
> *Worm nor snail do no offence.*

CHORUS

> *Philomel with melody, etc.*

TITANIA *sleeps.*

FIRST FAIRY

Hence away; now all is well;
One aloof stand sentinel.   25

Exeunt Fairies

Enter OBERON, *who puts the juice on* TITANIA'S *eyelids.*

28   *languish*   agonise over (as people in love do).

29   *ounce*   wild cat.

30   *Pard*   leopard.

31–2   *In thy eye ... dear*   when you wake up, whatever you see – even if it is vile and ugly – you will be in love with.

37   *tarry*   wait.

41   *troth*   promise to one another.

44   *sense*   meaning.

   innocence   innocent remarks.

45   *Love takes ... love's conference*   love understands the true meaning of conversations between lovers.

46   *knit*   completely united.

47   *but one*   only one.

OBERON

    What thou seest when thou dost wake,
    Do it for thy true love take:
    Love and languish for his sake.
    Be it ounce, or cat, or bear,
    Pard, or boar with bristled hair,   30
    In thy eye that shall appear,
    When thou wak'st, it is thy dear.
    Wake when some vile thing is near.

                                            Exit

Enter LYSANDER *and* HERMIA.

LYSANDER

    Fair love, you faint with wandering in the wood,
    And to speak truth, I have forgot our way.   35
    We'll rest us, Hermia, if you think it good,
    And tarry for the comfort of the day.

HERMIA

    Be it so, Lysander; find you out a bed,
    For I upon this bank will rest my head.

LYSANDER

    One turf shall serve as pillow for us both;   40
    One heart, one bed, two bosoms, and one troth.

HERMIA

    Nay, good Lysander; for my sake, my dear,
    Lie further off yet, do not lie so near.

LYSANDER

    O take the sense, sweet, of my innocence.
    Love takes the meaning in love's conference.   45
    I mean that my heart unto yours is knit,
    So that but one heart we can make of it.

48 *interchainéd*   linked.

51 *For lying ... not lie*   because sleeping here ('lying so'), I am not trying to deceive you ('I do not lie'). This word-play is called a pun.

52 *riddles very prettily*   plays with words in a clever and amusing way.

53 *beshrew my manners*   put a curse on me for being bad-mannered (for suggesting Lysander is lying).

62 *end ... loyalty*   may I die if I go against your wishes.

64 *With half ... pressed!*   Hermia returns Lysander's loving goodnight.

67 *approve*   test.

68 *force ... love*   power to awaken love.

70 *Weeds*   clothing.

Two bosoms interchainéd with an oath,
So then, two bosoms, and a single troth.
Then by your side no bed-room me deny,   50
For lying so, Hermia, I do not lie.

HERMIA

Lysander riddles very prettily;
Now much beshrew my manners and my pride,
If Hermia meant to say Lysander lied.
But, gentle friend, for love and courtesy   55
Lie further off, in human modesty;
Such separation as may well be said
Becomes a virtuous bachelor and a maid;
So far be distant, and good night, sweet friend:
Thy love ne'er alter, till thy sweet life end!   60

LYSANDER

Amen, amen, to that fair prayer say I;
And then, end life, when I end loyalty!
Here is my bed; sleep give thee all his rest.

HERMIA

With half that wish, the wisher's eyes be pressed!

They sleep. Enter PUCK.

PUCK

Through the forest have I gone,   65
But Athenian found I none
On whose eyes I might approve
This flower's force in stirring love.
Night and silence: who is here?
Weeds of Athens he doth wear: 70
This is he, my master said,
Despised the Athenian maid:
And here the maiden, sleeping sound,

74 *dank* unpleasantly damp.

 durst dares.

76 *lack-love* person lacking in loving feelings.

 kill-courtesy rude and uncivil.

77 *Churl* surly, ill-bred person.

78 *owe* own.

79–80 *let love ... thy eyelid* let love have such a powerful effect on you that you cannot sleep.

84 *charge thee hence* order you to go away.

 haunt follow.

85 *darkling* in the dark.

86 *Stay on thy peril* stay here at your own risk.

87 *fond* foolish.

88 *The more ... my grace* the more I plead, the less favour I receive from Demetrius.

95–6 *no marvel ... presence thus* no wonder that Demetrius runs away from me as if I were a monster.

On the dank and dirty ground.
Pretty soul, she durst not lie   75
Near this lack-love, this kill-courtesy.
Churl, upon thy eyes I throw
All the power this charm doth owe:
When thou wak'st let love forbid
Sleep his seat on thy eyelid.   80
So awake when I am gone;
For I must now to Oberon.

Exit

Enter DEMETRIUS *and* HELENA, *running*.

HELENA

Stay, though thou kill me, sweet Demetrius.

DEMETRIUS

I charge thee hence, and do not haunt me thus.

HELENA

O wilt thou darkling leave me? Do not so.   85

DEMETRIUS

Stay on thy peril; I alone will go.

Exit DEMETRIUS

HELENA

O, I am out of breath, in this fond chase,
The more my prayer, the lesser is my grace.
Happy is Hermia, wheresoe'er she lies,
For she hath blessèd and attractive eyes.   90
How came her eyes so bright? Not with salt tears:
If so, my eyes are oftener washed than hers.
No, no, I am as ugly as a bear;
For beasts that meet me run away for fear.
Therefore no marvel though Demetrius   95

69

97　*dissembling glass*　mirror that lies.

98　*sphery eyne*　star-eyes.

103　*Transparent*　gloriously beautiful (but Lysander carries on to use the more familiar sense of being able to be seen through).

art　magic.

104　*makes me see thy heart*　makes me see that you love me.

110　*repent*　regret.

114　*will*　desire.

reason　in this speech Lysander makes much of reason, ironically unaware that what he is feeling has nothing to do with it, and everything to do with Puck's magic flower. This links with other ironic references to rationality in love by the young lovers.

117　*So I ... reason*　until now, I have been too young to form a proper judgement.

118　*And touching ... skill*　and now that I have developed my full powers of judgement.

119　*marshall to my will*　commander of my desires.

120　*o'erlook*　observe.

122　*Wherefore*　why?

keen　sharp.

Do as a monster, fly my presence thus.
What wicked and dissembling glass of mine
Made me compare with Hermia's sphery eyne?
But who is here? Lysander on the ground!
Dead or asleep? I see no blood, no wound.   100
Lysander, if you live, good sir, awake!

LYSANDER (*awaking*)

And run through fire I will for thy sweet sake!
Transparent Helena! Nature shows art,
That through thy bosom makes me see thy heart.
Where is Demetrius? O how fit a word   105
Is that vile name, to perish on my sword!

HELENA

Do not say so, Lysander; say not so:
What though he love your Hermia? Lord, what
    though?
Yet Hermia still loves you; then be content.

LYSANDER

Content with Hermia? No, I do repent   110
The tedious minutes I with her have spent.
Not Hermia but Helena I love:
Who will not change a raven for a dove?
The will of man is by his reason swayed;
And reason says you are the worthier maid.   115
Things growing are not ripe until their season;
So I, being young, till now ripe not to reason;
And touching now the point of human skill,
Reason becomes the marshal to my will,
And leads me to your eyes, where I o'erlook   120
Love's stories, written in love's richest book.

HELENA

Wherefore was I to this keen mockery born?

127 *flout my insuffiency* make my inadequacies obvious.

128 *Good troth* indeed.

     good sooth really.

130 *perforce* indeed.

131 *gentleness* courtesy, behaviour suitable for a gentleman.

132 *of* by.

136 *surfeit* excess.

138–9 *the heresies ... deceive* false beliefs ('heresies') that people give up are hated most by those who used to believe in them most strongly.

140 *thou* you (i.e. my love for Hermia).

141 *Of* by.

142 *address ... might* devote all your efforts.

145 *crawling serpent* Hermia has been having a nightmare that a snake has been attacking her.

147 *quake* tremble.

148 *eat* ate.

149 *cruel prey* cruel attack.

150 *what, removed* what, has he gone away?

When at your hands did I deserve this scorn?
Is 't not enough, is 't not enough, young man,
That I did never, no, nor never can   125
Deserve a sweet look from Demetrius' eye,
But you must flout my insufficiency?
Good troth, you do me wrong, good sooth, you do,
In such disdainful manner me to woo.
But fare you well; perforce I must confess   130
I thought you lord of more true gentleness.
O, that a lady of one man refused
Should of another therefore be abused!

                                              Exit

LYSANDER

She sees not Hermia. Hermia, sleep thou there;
And never mayst thou come Lysander near.   135
For, as a surfeit of the sweetest things
The deepest loathing to the stomach brings,
Or as the heresies that men do leave,
Are hated most of those they did deceive;
So thou, my surfeit, and my heresy,   140
Of all be hated, but the most of me.
And, all my powers, address your love and might
To honour Helen, and to be her knight!

                                              Exit

HERMIA (*awaking*)

Help me, Lysander, help me! do thy best   *in dream*
To pluck this crawling serpent from my breast!   145
Ay me, for pity! what a dream was here!
Lysander, look, how I do quake with fear.
Methought a serpent eat my heart away,
And you sat smiling at his cruel prey.
Lysander! what, removed? Lysander! lord!   150

151 *out of hearing*   out of earshot.
154 *perceive you are not nigh*   come to the conclusion that you are not nearby.

What, out of hearing? Gone? No sound, no word?
Alack, where are you? Speak, and if you hear:
Speak, of all loves; I swoon almost with fear.
No? Then I will perceive you are not nigh.
Either death or you I'll find immediately.   155

Exit

☐ Act 3: summary

Bottom, Quince and their friends are rehearsing the play 'Pyramus and Thisby' in the woods, as they had planned. Puck chances upon them, and by magic, mischievously transforms Bottom's head into that of an ass. Bottom is unaware of what has happened but the sight of him makes the others run away in terror. Finding himself alone, Bottom sings to cheer himself up and this awakens Titania, who is sleeping nearby. She instantly falls in love with him, and tells her attendant fairies to satisfy his every whim. Bottom accepts all this cheerfully, and Titania leads him away to her bower.

Puck brings Oberon the news that Titania has fallen in love with Bottom, and that the young Athenian's eyes have been successfully smeared with the magic juice. Demetrius and Hermia enter, Demetrius having found her alone. He is still protesting love to her, but she accuses him of killing Lysander in his sleep – she cannot think of another reason why Lysander should desert her. She runs away and Demetrius, admitting defeat, lies down and sleeps.

It is now clear to Puck and Oberon that the wrong Athenian has been treated with the juice, so Oberon sends Puck to find Helena while he smears Demetrius' eyes. Helena enters with Lysander in hot pursuit still protesting love, which Helena still rejects as mockery. Their voices wake Demetrius, who duly falls in love with Helena. She cannot take this instant conversion seriously either and accuses them of conspiring with each other to humiliate her.

Hermia now enters, relieved to have found Lysander at last. He rejects her, telling her that it is now Helena that he loves. Helena assumes Hermia must be in on the conspiracy too, and a full-scale row develops with the men challenging one another to fight for Helena's love and the enraged Hermia trying to fight Helena for having lured Lysander away from her.

Oberon suspects Puck of having caused all this confusion for his own amusement, but Puck pleads innocence. Oberon instructs Puck to make sure Demetrius and Lysander do not harm each other while he makes his peace with

Lysander, Demetrius and Helena: London Bubble Theatre, 1988.

Titania. Puck makes the darkness still darker, and tires out the two Athenians by imitating their voices and leading them a dance through the woods. Eventually they sleep, as do the exhausted Helena and Hermia. Puck anoints Lysander's eyes with the juice of another herb which reverses the effect of the love potion, so that he will go back to loving Hermia.

2 *Pat, pat*   punctually, on the dot.

4 *hawthorn-brake*   hawthorn bush.

tiring-house   dressing room.

8 *bully*   my friend.

12 *abide*   tolerate.

13 *By 'r lakin*   by Our Lady, a mild swear word.

parlous   dangerous and difficult.

Act Three

Scene one

The same place.

TITANIA *sleeps. Enter* QUINCE, SNUG, BOTTOM, FLUTE, SNOUT *and* STARVELING.

BOTTOM

Are we all met?

QUINCE

Pat, pat; and here's a marvellous convenient place
for our rehearsal. This green plot shall be our
stage, this hawthorn-brake our tiring-house; and
we will do it in action, as we will do it before the   5
Duke.

BOTTOM

Peter Quince?

QUINCE

What sayest thou, bully Bottom?

BOTTOM

There are things in this comedy of Pyramus and
Thisby that will never please. First, Pyramus must   10
draw a sword to kill himself; which the ladies
cannot abide. How answer you that?

SNOUT

By 'r lakin, a parlous fear.

STARVELING

I believe we must leave the killing out, when all
is done.   15

16 *Not a whit*   not at all.

   device   solution.

17 *prologue*   introduction, to be spoken before the play starts.

19 *indeed*   really.

   for the more ... assurance   to reassure them further.

24 *eight and six*   lines of alternately eight syllables and six syllables.

27 *afeard*   afraid.

32 *fowl*   once again Bottom is getting confused as a lion is of course an animal not a bird.

BOTTOM

Not a whit; I have a device to make all well. Write
me a prologue, and let the prologue seem to say,
we will do no harm with our swords, and that
Pyramus is not killed indeed; and for the more
better assurance, tell them that I Pyramus am not   20
Pyramus, but Bottom the weaver; this will put
them out of fear.

QUINCE

Well, we will have such a prologue; and it shall be
written in eight and six.

BOTTOM

No, make it two more; let it be written in eight and   25
eight.

SNOUT

Will not the ladies be afeard of the lion?

STARVELING

I fear it, I promise you.

BOTTOM

Masters, you ought to consider with yourself, to
bring in, God shield us, a lion among ladies is a   30
most dreadful thing: for there is not a more fearful
wild fowl than your lion living; and we ought to
look to 't.

SNOUT

Therefore another prologue must tell he is not a
lion.   35

BOTTOM

Nay, you must name his name, and half his face
must be seen through the lion's neck; and he

39 *defect* Bottom means 'effect'.

42–3 *it were pity of my life* it would put my life at risk.

52–3 *find out moonshine* find out if the moon shines that night.

55 *casement* window.

57 *disfigure* Quince, like Bottom, has started to use the wrong word; he means figure or represent.

himself must speak through, saying thus, or to the
same defect: 'Ladies', or 'Fair ladies' 'I would wish
you' or 'I would request you', or 'I would entreat 40
you, not to fear, not to tremble: my life for yours.
If you think I come hither as a lion, it were pity
of my life. No, I am no such thing; I am a man
as other men are'; and there indeed let him name
his name, and tell them plainly he is Snug the 45
joiner.

QUINCE

Well, it shall be so: but there is two hard things,
that is, to bring the moonlight into a chamber;
for, you know, Pyramus and Thisby meet by
moonlight. 50

SNOUT

Doth the moon shine that night we play our play?

BOTTOM

A calendar, a calendar; look in the almanac; find
out moonshine, find out moonshine.

QUINCE

Yes, it doth shine that night.

BOTTOM

Why, then may you leave a casement of the great 55
chamber window, where we play, open, and the
moon may shine in at the casement.

QUINCE

Ay, or else one must come in with a bush of thorns
and a lantern, and say he comes to disfigure, or
to present, the person of moonshine. Then there 60
is another thing; we must have a wall in the great

66 *present Wall*   represent (the) Wall.

67 *loam*   mixture of clay, sand and straw, used for making bricks or plastering walls.

67–8 *roughcast*   mixture of lime and gravel used to plaster outside walls.

74 *that brake*   the hawthorn bush mentioned in line 4.

76 *hempen homespuns*   Puck refers to the players by the clothes they wear – home-made garments of coarse, hemp cloth.

77 *cradle*   bed.

78 *toward*   in preparation.

   auditor   members of the audience.

81 *odious*   loathsome. Bottom is corrected by Quince.

chamber; for Pyramus and Thisby, says the story, did talk through the chink of a wall.

SNOUT

You can never bring in a wall. What say you, Bottom?   65

BOTTOM

Some man or other must present Wall and let him have some plaster, or some loam, or some rough-cast about him, to signify wall; or let him hold his fingers thus; and through that cranny shall Pyramus and Thisby whisper.   70

QUINCE

If that may be, then all is well. Come, sit down, every mother's son, and rehearse your parts. Pyramus, you begin; when you have spoken your speech, enter into that brake; and so every one according to his cue.   75

Enter PUCK *behind.*

PUCK

What hempen home-spuns have we swaggering
     here,
So near the cradle of the Fairy Queen?
What, a play toward? I'll be an auditor;
An actor too, perhaps, if I see cause.

QUINCE

Speak, Pyramus. Thisby, stand forth.   80

BOTTOM *as* PYRAMUS

Thisby, the flowers of odious savours sweet.

QUINCE

Odours, odours.

89 *marry*   by the Virgin Mary, a mild swear word.

94 *Most brisky ... Jew*   line with little obvious meaning. A 'brisky juvenal' sounds like a healthy young man, while 'Jew' seems to be there for no other reason than to make the rhyme with 'hue' (line 92).

96 *Ninny's*   comic mistaken pronunciation of Ninus, king of Nineveh. A ninny is also a fool. Bottom and Flute continue to use words wrongly right to the end of the play.

BOTTOM *as* PYRAMUS

    Odours savours sweet;
    So hath thy breath, my dearest Thisby dear.
    But hark, a voice! stay thou but here a while,   85
    And by and by I will to thee appear.

                                                  Exit behind

PUCK

    A stranger Pyramus than e'er played here!

FLUTE

    Must I speak now?

QUINCE

    Ay, marry, must you; for you must understand, he
    goes but to see a noise that he heard, and is to 90
    come again.

FLUTE *as* THISBE

    Most radiant Pyramus, most lily-white of hue,
    Of colour like the red rose on triumphant brier,
    Most brisky juvenal, and eke most lovely Jew,
    As truest horse, that yet would never tire.   95
    I'll meet thee, Pyramus, at Ninny's tomb.

QUINCE

    Ninus' tomb, man! Why, you must not speak that
    yet; that you answer to Pyramus: you speak all
    your part at once, cues and all. Pyramus, enter:
    your cue is past; it is 'never tire'.   100

FLUTE *as* THISBE

    O, – As true as truest horse, that yet would never
    tire.

Re-enter BOTTOM *wearing an ass's head.*

102 *fair*   handsome.
   were   would be.
103 *We are haunted*   Quince takes fright and thinks Bottom is a ghost.
105 *about a round*   in a circle dance, or on a roundabout route.
106 *brake*   bushes.
111 *knavery*   cruel trick.
115–16 *an ass-head of your own*   Bottom is unaware of his appearance, of course.

BOTTOM *as* PYRAMUS

If I were fair, Thisby, I were only thine.

QUINCE

O monstrous! O strange! We are haunted; pray, masters, fly! masters, help!

Exeunt all but BOTTOM *and* PUCK

PUCK (*coming forward*)

I'll follow you, I'll lead you about a round,   105
Through bog, through bush, through brake, through brier;
Sometime a horse I'll be, sometime a hound,
A hog, a headless bear, sometime a fire;
And neigh, and bark, and grunt, and roar, and burn,
Like horse, hound, hog, bear, fire, at every turn. 110

Exit

BOTTOM

Why do they run away? This is a knavery of them to make me afeard.

Re-enter SNOUT.

SNOUT

O Bottom, thou art changed! What do I see on thee?

BOTTOM

What do you see? You see an ass-head of your 115 own, do you?

Exit SNOUT

Re-enter QUINCE.

117 *translated*   Quince means transformed.

118 *an ass of me*   the comic effect is gained by Bottom not realising what he looks like.

121 *that*   so that.

123 *ousel cock*   male blackbird.

125 *throstle*   thrush.

126 *little quill*   small, piping voice.

129 *plain-song*   simple chanting with a limited number of notes, like the cuckoo.

130–4 *Whose note ... never so?*   Bottom's point in these lines is that the cuckoo's song sounds like cuckold, a man whose wife has been unfaithful to him. Many men hear the bird calling them cuckolds, and are unable to deny it!

136 *enamoured of*   in love with.

137 *enthrallèd to thy shape*   held captive by your appearance.

138 *thy fair virtue's force*   the power of your beautiful nature.

  perforce   inevitably.

QUINCE

Bless thee Bottom, bless thee! thou art translated!

Exit

BOTTOM

I see their knavery: this is to make an ass of me,
to fright me, if they could; but I will not stir from
this place, do what they can. I will walk up and 120
down here, and I will sing, that they shall hear I
am not afraid. (*Sings.*)

The ousel cock, so black of hue,
With orange-tawny bill,
The throstle with his note so true,   125
The wren with little quill.

TITANIA (*awaking*)

What angel wakes me from my flowery bed?

BOTTOM (*sings*)

The finch, the sparrow, and the lark,
The plain-song cuckoo grey;
Whose note full many a man doth mark, 130
And dares not answer 'nay'.

For indeed, who would set his wit to so foolish a
bird? Who would give a bird the lie, though he cry
'cuckoo' never so?

TITANIA

I pray thee, gentle mortal, sing again;   135
Mine ear is much enamoured of thy note;
So is mine eye enthrallèd to thy shape;
And thy fair virtue's force perforce doth move me
On the first view, to say, to swear I love thee.

144 *gleek*   make jokes with a point.

146 *if I had wit enough*   if I had enough knowledge.

147 *serve my own turn*   answer my own needs.

151 *no common rate*   of no ordinary rank.

152 *still*   always.

tend upon my state   serve me as a queen.

155 *deep*   ocean.

157 *purge thy mortal grossness*   rid you of all the coarse, physical aspects of an earthly being.

BOTTOM

Methinks, mistress, you should have little reason 140
for that: and yet, to say the truth, reason and love
keep little company together nowadays. The more
the pity that some honest neighbours will not make
them friends. Nay, I can gleek upon occasion.

TITANIA

Thou art as wise as thou art beautiful.   145

BOTTOM

Not so, neither; but if I had wit enough to get out
of this wood, I have enough to serve mine own
turn.

TITANIA

Out of this wood do not desire to go;
Thou shalt remain here, whether thou wilt or no. 150
I am a spirit of no common rate;
The summer still doth tend upon my state,
And I do love thee; therefore, go with me.
I'll give thee fairies to attend on thee;
And they shall fetch thee jewels from the deep, 155
And sing, while thou on pressed flowers dost sleep:
And I will purge thy mortal grossness so
That thou shalt like an airy spirit go.
Peaseblossom, Cobweb, Moth, and Mustardseed!

Enter Four Fairies.

FIRST FAIRY

Ready

SECOND FAIRY

        And I.

162 *in his walks*   where he is walking.

    gambol in his eyes   dance before him.

163 *apricocks*   apricots.

    dewberries   blackberries.

165 *humble-bees*   bumble-bees.

166 *night-tapers*   candles.

    crop their waxen thighs   take wax from the bees' legs.

168 *To have ... arise*   to provide light for Bottom on his way to bed and when he gets up in the morning.

171 *do him courtesies*   show your respect by serving him.

173 *mercy*   thank you (from the French).

THIRD FAIRY

And I.

FOURTH FAIRY

And I.

ALL

Where shall we go? 160

TITANIA

Be kind and courteous to this gentleman;
Hop in his walks, and gambol in his eyes;
Feed him with apricocks and dewberries,
With purple grapes, green figs, and mulberries;
The honey-bags steal from the humble-bees,   165
And for night-tapers crop their waxen thighs,
And light them at the fiery glow-worm's eyes,
To have my love to bed, and to arise;
And pluck the wings from painted butterflies
To fan the moonbeams from his sleeping eyes;   170
Nod to him, elves, and do him courtesies.

FIRST FAIRY

Hail, mortal!

SECOND FAIRY

Hail!

THIRD FAIRY

Hail!

FOURTH FAIRY

Hail!

BOTTOM

I cry your worships mercy heartily; I beseech your
worship's name?

177–8 *if I cut ... you* in the country cobwebs were often used to cover cuts and grazes; 'make bold with' here means use.

179 *Peaseblossom* flower of a pea plant.

180 *Squash* unripe pea-pod.

181 *Peascod* ripe pea-pod.

185 *patience* suffering.

185–7 *Good Master ... house* Bottom is jokingly sympathising with Mustardseed, because so many of his relatives ('house') have been eaten with 'ox-beef'.

188–9 *your kindred ... ere now* your family have made me cry before now (i) because I'm sad that so many have been eaten and (ii) because strong mustard can make your eyes water.

191 *bower* Titania's sleeping place.

192–3 *The moon ... little flower* in Shakespeare's day, dew was thought to fall from the moon. Titania compares the dew falling with the moon weeping, and the dew-covered flowers look as if they have been weeping too.

195 *enforcéd chastity* this could mean either (i) the moon and flowers are crying because a virgin has been raped (which connects with Diana, the moon goddess also being the goddess of chastity) or (ii) that the cause for lamenting is that chastity has been forced on an unwilling woman (which goes well with what Titania is planning to do with Bottom in her bower).

FIRST FAIRY
Cobweb. 175

BOTTOM

I shall desire you of more acquaintance, good
Master Cobweb: if I cut my finger, I shall make
bold with you. Your name, honest gentleman?

SECOND FAIRY
Peaseblossom.

BOTTOM

I pray you, commend me to Mistress Squash, your 180
mother, and to Master Peascod, your father. Good
Master Peaseblossom, I shall desire you of more
acquaintance too. Your name, I beseech you, sir?

THIRD FAIRY
Mustardseed.

BOTTOM

Good Master Mustardseed, I know your patience 185
well: that same cowardly, giant-like ox-beef hath
devoured many a gentleman of your house. I
promise you, your kindred hath made my eyes
water ere now. I desire you of more acquaintance,
good Master Mustardseed. 190

TITANIA

Come, wait upon him, lead him to my bower.
The moon, methinks, looks with a watery eye,
And when she weeps, weeps every little flower,
Lamenting some enforcéd chastity.
Tie up my love's tongue, bring him silently. 195

Exeunt behind

1 *be awaked*   is awake.

2 *came in her eye*   she saw.

3 *dote on in extremity*   fall passionately in love with.

4 *How now*   what's the news?

5 *night-rule*   happenings in the night.

7 *close and consecrated*   secret and holy.

9 *patches*   fools.

  rude mechanicals   simple working men.

10 *upon Athenian stalls*   in the market places of Athens.

12 *nuptial-day*   wedding day.

13 *shallowest thick-skin ... sort*   most insensitive of this group of stupid men.

14 *presented*   represented.

  sport   play.

15 *Forsook*   left.

  entered in a brake   went behind a bush.

16 *advantage*   lucky chance.

17 *nole*   head.

18 *Anon ... answeréd*   soon his cue came to answer Thisbe.

19 *And forth ... comes*   and out comes the man I had disguised.

  spy   see.

20 *As wild geese ... eye*   like wild geese when they see a hunter creeping up on
   them.

21 *russet-pated ... sort*   grey-headed jackdaws, in large numbers.

22 *report*   sound of a gun firing.

23 *Sever themselves*   scatter.

24 *sight*   appearance.

Scene two

Another part of the wood.

Enter OBERON.

OBERON

I wonder if Titania be awaked;
Then, what it was that next came in her eye,
Which she must dote on in extremity.

Enter PUCK.

Here comes my messenger. How now, mad spirit!
What night-rule now about this haunted grove?   5

PUCK

My mistress with a monster is in love.
Near to her close and consecrated bower,
While she was in her dull and sleeping hour,
A crew of patches, rude mechanicals,
That work for bread upon Athenian stalls,   10
Were met together to rehearse a play
Intended for great Theseus' nuptial-day.
The shallowest thick-skin of that barren sort,
Who Pyramus presented, in their sport
Forsook his scene and entered in a brake;   15
When I did him at this advantage take,
An ass's nole I fixéd on his head.
Anon his Thisbe must be answeréd,
And forth my mimic comes. When they him spy,
As wild geese that the creeping fowler eye,   20
Or russet-pated choughs, many in sort,
Rising and cawing at the gun's report,
Sever themselves and madly sweep the sky,
So at his sight, away his fellows fly;

25 *at our stamp ... falls*   at the sound of our feet on the ground they ran off, tumbling over one another.

27 *lost with*   overcome by.

28 *senseless things*   things that are not alive.

wrong   injury.

29 *apparel*   clothing.

30 *from yielders all things catch*   take everything from those willing to give it up.

32 *translated*   turned into another shape.

36 *latched*   moistened.

38 *took*   caught.

40 *That*   so that.

of force   unavoidably.

eyed   seen.

41 *Stand close*   stay hidden.

44 *Lay breath*   use words.

45 *chide*   rebuke mildly.

And at our stamp here, o'er and o'er one falls;   25
He 'murder' cries, and help from Athens calls.
Their sense thus weak, lost with their fears thus
    strong,
Made senseless things begin to do them wrong;
For briers and thorns at their apparel snatch;
Some sleeves, some hats; from yielders all things
    catch.   30
I led them on in this distracted fear,
And left sweet Pyramus translated there;
When in that moment, so it came to pass,
Titania waked, and straightway loved an ass.

OBERON

This falls out better than I could devise.   35
But hast thou yet latched the Athenian's eyes
With the love-juice, as I did bid thee do?

PUCK

I took him sleeping – that is finished too –
And the Athenian woman by his side;
That, when he waked, of force she must be eyed.   40

Enter DEMETRIUS *and* HERMIA.

OBERON

Stand close: this is the same Athenian.

PUCK

This is the woman, but not this the man.

DEMETRIUS

O, why rebuke you him that loves you so?
Lay breath so bitter on your bitter foe.

HERMIA

Now I but chide, but I should use thee worse,   45

48 *Being o'er shoes ... deep*   since you are already up to your ankles in blood, you may as well plunge in further.

53–5 *This whole earth ... Antipodes*   a hole could be bored right through the earth, so that the moon could creep through it and shine at midday on the other side ('the Antipodes'), annoying the sun ('Her brother').

61 *Venus*   the planet, a bright star at evening or morning.

62 *to*   to do with.

64 *carcass*   dead body.

68 *once tell true*   for once, tell the truth.

69 *being awake*   when he was awake.

71 *worm*   snake.

For thou, I fear, hast given me cause to curse.
If thou hast slain Lysander in his sleep,
Being o'er shoes in blood, plunge in the deep,
And kill me too.
The sun was not so true unto the day   50
As he to me. Would he have stolen away
From sleeping Hermia? I'll believe as soon
This whole earth may be bored, and that the moon
May through the centre creep, and so displease
Her brother's noontide with the Antipodes.   55
It cannot be but thou hast murdered him;
So should a murderer look; so dead, so grim.

DEMETRIUS

So should the murdered look; and so should I,
Pierced through the heart with your stern cruelty:
Yet you, the murderer, look as bright, as clear   60
As yonder Venus in her glimmering sphere.

HERMIA

What's this to my Lysander? Where is he?
Ah, good Demetrius, wilt thou give him me?

DEMETRIUS

I had rather give his carcass to my hounds.

HERMIA

Out, dog! out, cur! thou drivest me past the
    bounds   65
Of maiden's patience. Hast thou slain him, then?
Henceforth be never numbered among men!
O, once tell true; tell true, even for my sake:
Durst thou have looked upon him, being awake?
And hast thou killed him sleeping? O brave touch! 70
Could not a worm, an adder do so much?

72 *adder*   the adder's tongue is forked ('double'), making it a symbol of deceit.

74 *misprised*   mistaken.

76 *vein*   mood.

84–5 *So sorrow's ... sorrow owe*   lack of sleep (caused by sorrow) and sorrow itself
have made Demetrius tired.

86–7 *Which now ... some stay*   sorrow will now pay back some of the lost sleep it
has caused, by making Demetrius feel sleepy now.

87 *tender*   payment.

make some stay   remain here.

88 *quite*   completely.

89 *true-love's sight*   the eyes of a faithful lover.

90 *Of your ... ensue*   from your mistake, it must inevitably result in.

91 *Some true love turned*   a faithful lover is turned against the one he loves. The
second meaning of the word 'turned' in this line is became.

An adder did it: for with doubler tongue
Than thine, thou serpent, never adder stung.

DEMETRIUS

You spend your passion on a misprised mood:
I am not guilty of Lysander's blood;   75
Nor is he dead, for aught that I can tell.

HERMIA

I pray thee tell me then that he is well.

DEMETRIUS

An if I could, what should I get therefore?

HERMIA

A privilege never to see me more.
And from thy hated presence part I so: 80
See me no more, whether he be dead or no.

Exit

DEMETRIUS

There is no following her in this fierce vein;
Here therefore for a while I will remain.
So sorrow's heaviness doth heavier grow
For debt that bankrupt sleep doth sorrow owe,   85
Which now in some slight measure it will pay,
If for his tender here I make some stay.

Lies down and sleeps.

OBERON

What hast thou done? Thou hast mistaken quite,
And laid the love-juice on some true-love's sight.
Of thy misprision must perforce ensue   90
Some true love turned, and not a false turned true.

92–3 *Then fate ... oath*   Puck is defending himself against Oberon's attack by saying that for every man that keeps his lover's vows ('holding troth'), a million more break them time after time.

96 *fancy-sick*   love-sick.

cheer   complexion.

97 *With sighs ... dear*   in Shakespeare's time it was believed that every time you sighed, you lost a drop of blood.

99 *against ... appear*   in preparation for her arrival.

101 *Tartar*   central Asian warrior.

104 *apple*   dead centre.

108 *by*   nearby.

112 *youth, mistook by me*   Lysander whom Puck mistook for Demetrius.

113 *lover's fee*   the reward of his love being returned.

114 *fond pageant*   foolish display.

PUCK

Then fate o'er-rules, that, one man holding troth,
A million fail, confounding oath on oath.

OBERON

About the wood go swifter than the wind,
And Helena of Athens look thou find.   95
All fancy-sick she is and pale of cheer
With sighs of love that cost the fresh blood dear.
By some illusion see thou bring her here;
I'll charm his eyes against she do appear.

PUCK

I go, I go, look how I go,   100
Swifter than arrow from the Tartar's bow.

Exit

OBERON

Flower of this purple dye,
Hit with Cupid's archery,
Sink in apple of his eye.
When his love he doth espy,   105
Let her shine as gloriously
As the Venus of the sky.
When thou wak'st, if she be by,
Beg of her for remedy.

Re-enter PUCK.

PUCK

Captain of our fairy band,   110
Helena is here at hand,
And the youth, mistook by me,
Pleading for a lover's fee.
Shall we their fond pageant see?
Lord, what fools these mortals be!   115

118 *at once*   at the same time.

119 *sport alone*   fun in its own right.

121 *befall preposterously*   turn out outrageously.

122 *woo in scorn*   pretend to love you in order to mock you.

125 *nativity*   birth, first appearance.

127 *badge of faith*   mark of truth. Lysander is referring to his tears, saying they are proof of the sincerity of his love.

128 *advance*   increase, and increasingly show.

129 *troth kills truth*   one vow (to Hermia) is cancelled by another (to Helena).

130 *give her o'er*   betray her.

131 *Weigh oath ... nothing weigh*   balance the oaths you made to Hermia against those you are now making to me, and you are left with nothing because they cancel each other out.

133 *tales*   lies.

OBERON

Stand aside: the noise they make
Will cause Demetrius to awake.

PUCK

Then will two at once woo one;
That must needs be sport alone;
And those things do best please me   120
That befall preposterously.

They stand behind.

Enter LYSANDER *and* HELENA.

LYSANDER

Why should you think that I should woo in scorn?
Scorn and derision never come in tears:
Look, when I vow I weep; and vows so born
In their nativity all truth appears.   125
How can these things in me seem scorn to you,
Bearing the badge of faith to prove them true?

HELENA

You do advance your cunning more and more.
When troth kills truth, O devilish-holy fray!
These vows are Hermia's: will you give her o'er? 130
Weigh oath with oath, and you will nothing weigh.
Your vows to her and me, put in two scales,
Will even weigh; and both as light as tales.

LYSANDER

I had no judgement when to her I swore.

HELENA

Nor none, in my mind, now you give her o'er.   135

LYSANDER

Demetrius loves her, and he loves not you.

138 *eyne* eyes.

139 *in show* in appearance.

141–3 *That pure ... thy hand* the snow on the high mountains of Turkey ('Taurus') seems black ('turn to a crow') in comparison with your hand. (Pale skin was considered a mark of beauty in Shakespeare's time.)

145 *bent* determined.

151 *in show* in appearance.

153 *superpraise my parts* overpraise my qualities.

157 *trim* fine (meant ironically).

159 *sort* birth.

160–1 *extort ... you sport* rob me of my calm just for you to have a bit of fun at my expense.

DEMETRIUS (*awaking*)

O Helen, goddess, nymph, perfect, divine,
To what, my love, shall I compare thine eyne?
Crystal is muddy: O how ripe in show
Thy lips, those kissing cherries, tempting grow!   140
That pure congealéd white, high Taurus' snow,
Fanned with the eastern wind, turns to a crow
When thou hold'st up thy hand. O let me kiss
This princess of pure white, this seal of bliss!

HELENA

O spite! O hell! I see you all are bent   145
To set against me for your merriment:
If you were civil, and knew courtesy,
You would not do me thus much injury.
Can you not hate me, as I know you do,
But you must join in souls to mock me too?   150
If you were men, as men you are in show,
You would not use a gentle lady so;
To vow, and swear, and superpraise my parts,
When I am sure you hate me with your hearts.
You both are rivals, and love Hermia;   155
And now both rivals, to mock Helena.
A trim exploit, a manly enterprise,
To conjure tears up in a poor maid's eyes
With your derision! None of noble sort
Would so offend a virgin, and extort   160
A poor soul's patience, all to make you sport.

LYSANDER

You are unkind, Demetrius; be not so;
For you love Hermia; this you know I know;
And here with all good will, with all my heart,
In Hermia's love I yield you up my part;   165

111

166 *bequeath* hand over.

171 *as guest-wise sojourned* stayed with her for a short while, like a guest.

174 *Disparage not* do not belittle.

175 *aby it dear* pay for it dearly.

177 *from the eye ... takes* robs the eye of its ability to see.

178 *quick of apprehension* sensitive.

179–80 *Wherein ... recompense* while it impares the sense of sight, it makes the sense of hearing twice as acute.

184 *press* urge.

112

And yours of Helena to me bequeath,
Whom I do love, and will do till my death.

HELENA

Never did mockers waste more idle breath.

DEMETRIUS

Lysander, keep thy Hermia; I will none.
If e'er I loved her, all that love is gone.   170
My heart to her but as guest-wise sojourned,
And now to Helen is it home returned,
There to remain.

LYSANDER

                          Helen, it is not so.

DEMETRIUS

Disparage not the faith thou dost not know,
Lest to thy peril thou aby it dear.   175
Look where thy love comes; yonder is thy dear.

Enter HERMIA.

HERMIA

Dark night, that from the eye his function takes,
The ear more quick of apprehension makes;
Wherein it doth impair the seeing sense,
It pays the hearing double recompense.   180
Thou art not by mine eye, Lysander, found;
Mine ear, I thank it, brought me to thy sound.
But why unkindly didst thou leave me so?

LYSANDER

Why should he stay whom love doth press to go?

HERMIA

What love could press Lysander from my side?   185

186 *bide*   remain where he was.

187 *engilds*   makes shine.

188 *yon fiery ... light*   stars. 'Oes' are orbs and also spangles.

192 *confederacy*   plot.

193 *conjoined*   got together.

194 *fashion*   make.

    in spite of me   to spite, or annoy me.

197 *bait*   tease.

198 *counsel*   confidences.

200 *chid ... parting us*   scolded time for going so fast when we were together, and forcing us to part.

203 *artificial*   skilled in making things.

205 *sampler*   piece of decorative embroidery.

208 *incorporate*   with one body.

210 *an union in partition*   a single person in two bodies.

213–14 *Two of ... one crest*   a complicated image from heraldry and coats of arms. Although the design on the shield may be in two halves, the whole design is unified by 'one crest', and is the property of ('due to') a single person. So, like Hermia and Helena, it is two things and one at the same time.

LYSANDER

Lysander's love, that would not let him bide;
Fair Helena, who more engilds the night
Than all yon fiery oes and eyes of light.
Why seek'st thou me? Could not this make thee
    know
The hate I bare thee made me leave thee so?   190

HERMIA

You speak not as you think; it cannot be.

HELENA

Lo, she is one of this confederacy!
Now I perceive they have conjoined, all three,
To fashion this false sport in spite of me.
Injurious Hermia, most ungrateful maid!   195
Have you conspired, have you with these contrived
To bait me with this foul derision?
Is all the counsel that we two have shared,
The sisters' vows, the hours that we have spent,
When we have chid the hasty-footed time   200
For parting us, – O, is all forgot?
All school-days' friendship, childhood innocence?
We, Hermia, like two artificial gods,
Have with our needles created both one flower,
Both on one sampler, sitting on one cushion,   205
Both warbling of one song, both in one key;
As if our hands, our sides, voices, and minds
Had been incorporate. So we grew together,
Like to a double cherry, seeming parted,
But yet an union in partition,   210
Two lovely berries, moulded on one stem;
So, with two seeming bodies, but one heart;
Two of the first, like coats in heraldry,
Due but to one and crownéd with one crest.

215 *rent* tear.

asunder apart.

227 *celestial* heavenly.

Wherefore why.

230 *tender* offer.

forsooth! indeed!

231 *But by your setting on* except through your encouragement.

232 *grace* favour.

234 *miserable most* the most miserable of women.

237 *perséver* carry on.

counterfeit put on falsely.

238 *Make mouths upon me* pull faces at me.

239 *hold the sweet jest up* carry on with your nice little joke (meant very sarcastically).

240 *chronicled* written about.

242 *argument* object of cruel entertainment.

And will you rent our ancient love asunder,   215
To join with men in scorning your poor friend?
It is not friendly, 't is not maidenly.
Our sex, as well as I, may chide you for it,
Though I alone do feel the injury.

HERMIA

I am amazéd at your passionate words;   220
I scorn you not; it seems that you scorn me.

HELENA

Have you not set Lysander, as in scorn,
To follow me, and praise my eyes and face?
And made your other love, Demetrius,
Who even but now did spurn me with his foot,   225
To call me goddess, nymph, divine, and rare,
Precious, celestial? Wherefore speaks he this
To her he hates? And wherefore doth Lysander
Deny your love, so rich within his soul,
And tender me, forsooth! affection,   230
But by your setting on, by your consent?
What though I be not so in grace as you,
So hung upon with love, so fortunate?
But miserable most, to love unloved.
This you should pity rather than despise.   235

HERMIA

I understand not what you mean by this.

HELENA

Ay, do, perséver, counterfeit sad looks,
Make mouths upon me when I turn my back,
Wink each at other, hold the sweet jest up:
This sport, well carried, shall be chronicled.   240
If you have any pity, grace, or manners,
You would not make me such an argument.

248 *If she ... compel*   if she can't change you by words ('entreat'), then I can do it by force ('compel').

255 *withdraw and prove it too*   let's go and fight it out.

256 *whereto tends all this?*   what does all this mean?

257 *Ethiope*   an insulting reference to Hermia's dark complexion. Elizabethan men favoured pale skin and fair hair in women.

But fare ye well; 't is partly mine own fault,
Which death or absence soon shall remedy.

LYSANDER

Stay, gentle Helena, hear my excuse; 245
My love, my life, my soul, fair Helena!

HELENA

O, excellent!

HERMIA

Sweet, do not scorn her so.

DEMETRIUS

If she cannot entreat, I can compel.

LYSANDER

Thou canst compel no more than she entreat.
Thy threats have no more strength than her weak
prayers. 250
Helen, I love thee, by my life I do;
I swear by that which I will lose for thee
To prove him false that says I love thee not.

DEMETRIUS

I say I love thee more than he can do.

LYSANDER

If thou say so, withdraw and prove it too. 255

DEMETRIUS

Quick, come.

HERMIA

Lysander, whereto tends all this?

LYSANDER

Away, you Ethiope.

258–9 *Seem to ... go!*   Demetrius accuses Lysander of pretending to want to fight, but avoiding actually fighting. This makes him a coward ('tame man'). In fact Hermia is preventing Lysander from leaving.

260 *burr*   seed head with little hooks that make it stick to clothing.

263 *tawny*   another insulting reference to Hermia's dark complexion.

Tartar   the Tartars from central Asia were famed as fighters as well as having dark skins.

264 *loathéd*   hated and despised.

265 *sooth*   really, indeed.

267 *bond*   signed contract.

268 *weak bond*   meaning Hermia.

DEMETRIUS

　　　　　No, no, sir,
Seem to break loose; take on as you would follow,
But yet come not; you are a tame man, go!

LYSANDER (*struggling with* HERMIA)

Hang off, thou cat, thou burr; vile thing, let loose, 260
Or I will shake thee from me like a serpent!

HERMIA

Why are you grown so rude? What change is this,
Sweet love?

LYSANDER

　　　　　Thy love? out, tawny Tartar, out!
Out, loathéd medicine; hated potion, hence!

HERMIA

Do you not jest?

HELENA

　　　　　Yes, sooth, and so do you.　　　265

LYSANDER

Demetrius, I will keep my word with thee.

DEMETRIUS

I would I had your bond; for I perceive
A weak bond holds you; I'll trust your word.

LYSANDER

What, should I hurt her, strike her, kill her dead?
Although I hate her, I'll not harm her so.　　　270

HERMIA

What, can you do me greater harm than hate?
Hate me? Wherefore? O me, what news, my love!
Am not I Hermia? Are not you Lysander?

274   *erewhile*   before, a while ago.

275   *Since night*   since the beginning of the night.

277   *In earnest*   seriously, not as a joke.

282   *juggler*   trickster.

canker-blossom   grub that ruins flowers.

288   *puppet*   many of the insults heaped on Hermia in this scene refer to her shortness of stature.

291   *urged her height*   used her superior height to win Lysander's love from her.

296   *painted*   using cosmetics to improve her complexion.

maypole   Hermia returns the insults about height by comparing Helena to the tall, thin poles danced around on May Day.

I am as fair now as I was erewhile.
Since night you loved me; yet since night you left
   me.   275
Why then, you left me – O, the gods forbid! –
In earnest, shall I say?

LYSANDER

               Ay, by my life:
And never did desire to see thee more.
Therefore be out of hope, of question, of doubt;
Be certain, nothing truer, 't is no jest   280
That I do hate thee, and love Helena.

HERMIA

O me! you juggler, you canker-blossom,
You thief of love! What, have you come by night
And stolen my love's heart from him?

HELENA

                  Fine, i' faith'!
Have you no modesty, no maiden shame,   285
No touch of bashfulness? What, will you tear
Impatient answers from my gentle tongue?
Fie, fie, you counterfeit, you puppet, you!

HERMIA

Puppet? why so! Ay, that way goes the game.
Now I perceive that she hath made compare   290
Between our statures; she hath urged her height,
And with her personage, her tall personage,
Her height, forsooth, she hath prevailed with him.
And are you grown so high in his esteem
Because I am so dwarfish and so low?   295
How low am I, thou painted maypole? Speak,
How low am I? I am not yet so low
But that my nails can reach unto thine eyes.

300   *curst*   bad-tempered.

301   *shrewishness*   quarrelling and insulting people.

302   *right*   proper.

304   *something*   somewhat.

308   *counsels*   secrets.

312   *chid me hence*   roughly ordered me to go away from here.

314   *so*   if.

317   *fond*   foolish.

HELENA

I pray you, though you mock me, gentlemen,
Let her not hurt me. I was never curst;   300
I have no gift at all in shrewishness;
I am a right maid for my cowardice;
Let her not strike me: you perhaps may think,
Because she is something lower than myself,
That I can match her.

HERMIA

               'Lower'! hark, again!   305

HELENA

Good Hermia, do not be so bitter with me.
I evermore did love you, Hermia,
Did ever keep your counsels, never wronged you;
Save that, in love unto Demetrius,
I told him of your stealth unto this wood.   310
He followed you; for love I followed him;
But he hath chid me hence and threatened me
To strike me, spurn me, nay, to kill me too.
And now, so you will let me quiet go,
To Athens will I bear my folly back,   315
And follow you no further. Let me go.
You see how simple and how fond I am.

HERMIA

Why, get you gone! who is 't that hinders you?

HELENA

A foolish heart, that I leave here behind.

HERMIA

What, with Lysander?

HELENA

              With Demetrius.   320

323 *keen and shrewd*   sharp and malicious.

327 *suffer her to flout me*   allow her to insult me.

329 *minimus*   (Latin) smallest.

knot-grass   low-growing grass. An extract of it was given to dwarves kept as entertainers by rulers, to stunt their growth.

330 *officious*   keen to do your duty.

333–5 *For if...aby it*   for if you show her that you feel the slightest affection for her, you will pay for it ('aby it').

336 *try*   put to the trial (i.e. by fighting).

338 *cheek by jowl*   side by side.

LYSANDER

Be not afraid, she shall not harm thee, Helena.

DEMETRIUS

No, sir, she shall not, though you take her part.

HELENA

O, when she's angry, she is keen and shrewd.
She was a vixen when she went to school;
And though she be but little, she is fierce.   325

HERMIA

Little again? nothing but low and little?
Why will you suffer her to flout me thus?
Let me come to her.

LYSANDER

              Get you gone, you dwarf,
You minimus, of hindering knot-grass made,
You bead, you acorn.

DEMETRIUS

              You are too officious   330
In her behalf that scorns your services.
Let her alone; speak not of Helena;
Take not her part. For if thou dost intend
Never so little show of love to her,
Thou shalt aby it.

LYSANDER

            Now she holds me not.   335
Now follow, if thou dar'st, to try whose right,
Of thine or mine, is most in Helena.

DEMETRIUS

Follow? Nay, I'll go with thee cheek by jowl.

                Exeunt LYSANDER *and* DEMETRIUS

341 *curst* bad-tempered.

342 *quicker for a fray* more eager for a fight.

345 *This is ... mistak'st* this is the result of your carelessness; you are always making mistakes.

346 *Or else ... wilfully* or else you do your mischief on purpose.

347 *mistook* made a mistake.

350 *enterprise* work.

352 *So did sort* turned out like this.

353 *jangling* quarrelling.

esteem a sport think that it is good entertainment.

355 *Hie* go.

overcast cover with clouds.

356 *welkin* sky.

anon at once.

357 *Acheron* black river in Hades, the ancient Greeks' name for hell.

358 *testy* bad-tempered.

HERMIA

You, mistress, all this coil is 'long of you.
Nay, go not back.

HELENA

              I will not trust you, I   340
Nor longer stay in your curst company.
Your hands than mine are quicker for a fray,
My legs are longer, though, to run away.

Exit

HERMIA

I am amazed, and know not what to say.

Exit

OBERON *and* PUCK *come forward.*

OBERON

This is thy negligence; still thou mistak'st;   345
Or else committ'st thy knaveries wilfully.

PUCK

Believe me, king of shadows, I mistook.
Did not you tell me I should know the man
By the Athenian garments he had on?
And so far blameless proves my enterprise   350
That I have 'nointed an Athenian's eyes;
And so far am I glad it so did sort,
As this their jangling I esteem a sport.

OBERON

Thou seest these lovers seek a place to fight.
Hie, therefore, Robin, overcast the night;   355
The starry welkin cover thou anon
With drooping fog as black as Acheron;
And lead these testy rivals so astray

359 *As* so that.

360 *Like to ... tongue* sometimes make your voice sound like Lysander's.

362 *rail* insult.

364 *death-counterfeiting* death-like.

365 *batty* bat-like.

367 *virtuous property* power to do good.

369 *wonted* usual, how they normally are.

370 *derision* insulting of one another.

372 *wend* go.

373 *With league ... never end* with a union that will not be broken until they die (i.e. a marriage contract).

376 *charméd* bewitched (Titania is still in love with Bottom, the 'monster').

379 *full* very.

380 *Aurora's harbinger* the morning star, the sign that the dawn is approaching. Aurora was the Roman goddess of the dawn.

381–7 *ghosts wandering ... night* Puck speaks of two sorts of ghosts in these lines. First, ordinary ghosts which roam about at night and then return to churchyards at dawn. Second, the 'Damnéd spirits', the ghosts of people who committed suicide. These are buried at crossroads ('crossways') or in rivers ('floods').

386 *They wilfully ... light* they keep themselves away from light on purpose.

387 *for aye consort with* live with for ever.

As one come not within another's way.
Like to Lysander sometime frame thy tongue,   360
Then stir Demetrius up with bitter wrong;
And sometime rail thou like Demetrius;
And from each other look thou lead them thus,
Till o'er their brows death-counterfeiting sleep
With leaden legs and batty wings doth creep;   365

Then crush this herb into Lysander's eye;
Whose liquor hath this virtuous property,
To take from thence all error with his might
And make his eyeballs roll with wonted sight.
When they next wake, all this derision   370
Shall seem a dream, and fruitless vision;
And back to Athens shall the lovers wend,
With league whose date till death shall never end.
Whiles I in this affair do thee employ,
I'll to my Queen, and beg her Indian boy;   375
And then I will her charméd eye release
From monster's view, and all things shall be peace.

PUCK

My fairy lord, this must be done with haste,
For night's swift dragons cut the clouds full fast,
And yonder shines Aurora's harbinger;   380
At whose approach, ghosts wandering here and
    there,
Troop home to churchyards. Damnéd spirits all,
That in crossways and floods have burial,
Already to their wormy beds are gone;
For fear lest day should look their shames upon,   385
They wilfully themselves exile from light,
And must for aye consort with black-browed night.

OBERON

But we are spirits of another sort:

131

389–93 *I with ... streams*   in these lines Oberon points out that like innocent, not
damned spirits, he has often enjoyed the sight of the dawn.

390 *groves*   woods.

391 *eastern gate*   where the sun rises.

392 *Neptune*   god of the ocean, here meaning the ocean itself.

395 *effect*   complete.

402 *drawn and ready*   with his sword drawn, ready to fight.

403 *straight*   immediately.

404 *plainer*   flatter and clearer.

I with the morning's love have oft made sport,
And, like a forester, the groves may tread   390
Even till the eastern gate, all fiery-red,
Opening on Neptune, with fair bléssed beams
Turns into yellow gold his salt green streams.
But notwithstanding, haste, make no delay:
We may effect this business yet ere day.   395

Exit OBERON

PUCK

Up and down, up and down,
I will lead them up and down;
I am feared in field and town;
Goblin, lead them up and down.
Here comes one.   400

Enter LYSANDER.

LYSANDER

Where art thou, proud Demetrius? Speak thou
now.

PUCK (*as* DEMETRIUS)
Here villain, drawn and ready. Where art thou?

LYSANDER
I will be with thee straight.

PUCK (*as* DEMETRIUS)
                          Follow me, then,
To plainer ground.

Exit LYSANDER

Enter DEMETRIUS.

DEMETRIUS
                          Lysander, speak again;

409 *recreant* cowardly traitor.
412 *try no manhood* not put our courage to the test.
415 *lighter-heeled* faster on his feet.

134

Thou runaway, thou coward, art thou fled?   405
Speak! In some bush? Where dost thou hide thy
   head?

PUCK (*as* LYSANDER)
Thou coward, art thou bragging to the stars,
Telling the bushes that thou look'st for wars,
And wilt not come? Come, recreant, come, thou
   child;
I'll whip thee with a rod. He is defiled   410
That draws a sword on thee.

DEMETRIUS
                    Yea, art thou there?

PUCK (*as* LYSANDER)
Follow my voice; we'll try no manhood here.

                                Exeunt

Re-enter LYSANDER.

LYSANDER
He goes before me, and still dares me on;
When I come where he calls, then he is gone.
The villain is much lighter-heeled than I: 415
I followed fast, but faster he did fly,
That fallen am I in dark uneven way,
And here will rest me. Come, thou gentle day;

Lies down.

For if but once thou show me thy grey light,
I'll find Demetrius, and revenge this spite. (*Sleeps*) 420

Re-enter PUCK *and* DEMETRIUS

PUCK (*as* LYSANDER)
Ho, ho, ho! coward, why com'st thou not?

422 *Abide me*   wait for me.

     wot   know.

426 *buy this dear*   pay dearly for this.

428 *constraineth*   forces.

429 *To measure ... cold bed*   to lie full stretch on the ground.

430 *By day's ... visited*   when the day breaks except to see me.

432 *Abate*   shorten.

439 *curst*   cross.

DEMETRIUS

Abide me, if thou dar'st; for well I wot,
Thou runn'st before me, shifting every place,
And dar'st not stand, nor look me in the face.
Where art thou now?

PUCK (*as* LYSANDER)

Come hither, I am here.   425

DEMETRIUS

Nay, then, thou mock'st me; thou shalt buy this
    dear,
If ever I thy face by daylight see.
Now, go thy way: faintness constraineth me
To measure out my length on this cold bed:
By day's approach look to be visited.   430

Lies down and sleeps.

Enter HELENA.

HELENA

O weary night, O long and tedious night,
Abate thy hours, shine comforts from the east,
That I may back to Athens by daylight.
From these that my poor company detest;
And sleep, that sometimes shuts up sorrow's eye,   435
Steal me awhile from mine own company.

Lies down and sleeps.

PUCK

Yet but three? Come one more.
Two of both kinds makes up four.
Here she comes, curst and sad;
Cupid is a knavish lad,   440
Thus to make poor females mad.

443 *Bedabbled* sprinkled.

445 *My legs ... desires* my legs will no longer do what I want them to.

447 *if they mean a fray* if Lysander and Demetrius mean to fight.

Enter HERMIA.

HERMIA
Never so weary, never so in woe,
Bedabbled with the dew, and torn with briers,
I can no further crawl, no further go;
My legs can keep no pace with my desires.   445
Here will I rest me till the break of day.
Heavens shield Lysander, if they mean a fray!

Lies down and sleeps.

PUCK
On the ground
Sleep sound;
I'll apply   450
To your eye,
Gentle lover, remedy. (*Squeezes the juice on*
LYSANDER'S *eyes*)
When thou wak'st,
Thou tak'st
True delight   455
In the sight
Of thy former lady's eye;
And the country proverb known,
That every man should take his own,
In your waking shall be shown.   460
Jack shall have Jill;
Nought shall go ill;
The man shall have his mare again, and all shall
    be well.

Exit

The lovers lie asleep.

Louise Gold as Titania: the New Shakespeare Company at the Open Air Theatre, Regent's Park, 1991 (photograph © Alastair Muir).

Act 4: summary

Bottom is having the time of his life in Titania's bower, waited on hand and foot by fairies and caressed and adored by Titania herself. They sleep, and Oberon, who has been watching, tells Puck that because Titania has now given up the little Indian boy, she can be released from the spell. He does this and she wakes up, horrified to see the grotesque creature she had been in love with. Oberon and Titania settle their differences, and Puck removes the ass head from the still-sleeping Bottom.

Theseus and Hippolyta enter with Egeus. They have been performing the ceremonies of May Day morning and now plan to go hunting with hounds. Egeus discovers his daughter Hermia asleep on the ground, and then sees Lysander, Demetrius and Helena too. Theseus asks for an explanation, and Egeus angrily demands his rights under the law – that he should decide who is to marry his daughter. Demetrius tells him that he no longer wants to marry Hermia because he is now in love with Helena, and Theseus decides that because the two couples are now neatly sorted out, he will override Egeus and allow Hermia and Lysander to marry. Theseus, Hippolyta and Egeus leave, and the lovers discuss the events of the night. Was it all a dream, they wonder? They leave, still half-believing that it was.

All this time Bottom has been sleeping on peacefully, but he now wakes up and is just as confused as the lovers about what went on during the night. Back in Athens, Quince and the other actors are depressed that with Bottom missing, they will not be able to put on their play before the Duke. But to their surprise and delight, Bottom arrives and tells them to get ready because their play is on the shortlist for the evening's entertainments.

2 *amiable* lovable.

  coy caress.

13 *fret* trouble.

16 *loth* unhappy, unwilling.

  overflown soaked and covered.

Act Four

Scene one

The same place.

Enter TITANIA *and* BOTTOM, *with the fairies attending, and*
OBERON *behind, unseen.*

TITANIA
  Come, sit thee down upon this flowery bed,
  While I thy amiable cheeks do coy,
  And stick musk-roses in thy sleek smooth head,
  And kiss thy fair large ears, my gentle joy.

BOTTOM
  Where's Peaseblossom?   5

PEASEBLOSSOM
  Ready.

BOTTOM
  Scratch my head, Peaseblossom. Where's Monsieur
  Cobweb?

COBWEB
  Ready.

BOTTOM
  Monsieur Cobweb, good monsieur, get you your   10
  weapons in your hand, and kill me a red-hipped
  humble-bee on the top of a thistle; and good
  monsieur, bring me the honey-bag. Do not fret
  yourself too much in the action, monsieur; and
  good monsieur, have a care the honey-bag break   15
  not; I would be loth to have you overflown with

20 *neaf* hand.

21 *leave your curtsy* stop bowing to me.

22 *What's your will?* what would you like me to do?

23 *Cavalery* Bottom's attempt at saying *cavaliere*, the Italian version of the English word cavalier.

24 *Cobweb* it was in fact Peaseblossom who was ordered to scratch. The mistake could be Bottom's or Shakespeare's.

25 *marvellous* remarkably.

30 *tongs and the bones* simple musical instruments. The tongs were a kind of triangle, and the bones were used to produce a rattling noise.

32 *peck of provender* helping of fodder such as hay or corn.

34 *bottle* bundle.

35 *fellow* equal.

a honey-bag, signior. Where's Monsieur Mustardseed?

MUSTARDSEED

Ready.

BOTTOM

Give my your neaf, Monsieur Mustardseed. Pray 20
you, leave your curtsy, good monsieur.

MUSTARDSEED

What's your will?

BOTTOM

Nothing, good monsieur, but to help Cavalery
Cobweb to scratch. I must to the barber's,
monsieur, for methinks I am marvellous hairy 25
about the face. And I am such a tender ass, if my
hair do but tickle me, I must scratch.

TITANIA

What, wilt thou hear some music, my sweet love?

BOTTOM

I have a reasonable good ear in music. Let's have
the tongs and the bones. 30

TITANIA

Or say, sweet love, what thou desirest to eat.

BOTTOM

Truly, a peck of provender; I could munch your
good dry oats. Methinks I have a great desire to
a bottle of hay: good hay, sweet hay, hath no
fellow. 35

TITANIA

I have a venturous fairy, that shall seek

40 *exposition*   Bottom means disposition, or urge.

42 *be all ways away*   leave in different directions.

45 *Enrings*   winds round.

   barky fingers   branches.

48 *dotage*   infatuation.

49 *of late*   recently.

50 *sweet favours*   flowers.

51 *upbraid*   rebuke, tell off.

55 *Was wont to*   used to.

   orient   from the east.

60 *changeling child*   the Indian boy who is the cause of the dispute between Oberon and Titania.

The squirrel's hoard, and fetch thee thence new
   nuts.

BOTTOM

I had rather have a handful or two of dried peas.
But I pray you, let none of your people stir me;
I have an exposition of sleep come upon me.   40

TITANIA

Sleep thou, and I will wind thee in my arms.
Fairies, be gone, and be all ways away.

Exeunt Fairies

So doth the woodbine the sweet honeysuckle
Gently entwist; the female ivy so
Enrings the barky fingers of the elm.   45
O, how I love thee! how I dote on thee!

They sleep.

Enter PUCK.

OBERON (*coming forward*)

Welcome, good Robin: seest thou this sweet sight?
Her dotage now I do begin to pity;
For meeting her of late behind the wood,
Seeking sweet favours for this hateful fool,   50
I did upbraid her, and fall out with her.
For she his hairy temples then had rounded
With coronet of fresh and fragrant flowers;
And that same dew, which sometime on the buds
Was wont to swell like round and orient pearls,   55
Stood now within the pretty flowerets' eyes
Like tears that did their own disgrace bewail.
When I had at my pleasure taunted her,
And she in mild terms begged my patience,
I then did ask of her her changeling child;   60

61 *straight* immediately.

65 *transforméd scalp* Oberon means the ass's head which has altered Bottom's appearance.

66 *swain* young man.

67 *when the other do* at the same time as the lovers.

68 *repair* return.

69 *accidents* events.

72 *wast wont* was accustomed.

74 *Dian's bud* the herb Oberon has for reversing the love potion ('Cupid's flower'), Diana being the goddess of chastity.

78 *Methought ... ass* I thought I was in love with an ass.

82–3 *strike ... sense* Oberon is calling on Puck to put the four lovers and Bottom into an even deeper sleep than they are in at the moment.

Which straight she gave me, and her fairy sent
To bear him to my bower in fairy land.
And now I have the boy, I will undo
This hateful imperfection of her eyes.
And, gentle Puck, take this transforméd scalp,   65
From off the head of this Athenian swain,
That he awaking when the other do,
May all to Athens back again repair,
And think no more of this night's accidents
But as the fierce vexation of a dream.   70
But first I will release the Fairy Queen.

Touches TITANIA'*s eyelids.*

        Be as thou wast wont to be;
        See as thou wast wont to see.
        Dian's bud o'er Cupid's flower
        Hath such force and blessed power.   75
Now, my Titania, wake you, my sweet Queen.

TITANIA (*wakes and rises*)
My Oberon! What visions have I seen!
Methought I was enamoured of an ass.

OBERON
There lies your love.

TITANIA
             How came these things to pass?
O, how mine eyes do loathe his visage now!   80

OBERON
Silence awhile. Robin, take off this head;
Titania, music call, and strike more dead
Than common sleep, of all these five the sense.

87 *rock the ground* make the ground rock like a cradle with their dancing.
88 *new in amity* have rediscovered our friendship.
98 *compass* encompass, go round.

TITANIA

Music, ho music, such as charmeth sleep!

Music plays.

PUCK

Now, when thou wak'st, with thine own fool's eyes
    peep.   85

OBERON

Sound, music; come, my Queen take hands with
    me,
And rock the ground whereon these sleepers be.
Now thou and I are new in amity,
And will tomorrow midnight solemnly
Dance in Duke Theseus' house triumphantly,   90
And bless it to all fair prosperity.
There shall the pairs of faithful lovers be
Wedded, with Theseus, all in jollity.

PUCK

Fairy King, attend and mark;
I do hear the morning lark.   95

OBERON

Then, my Queen, in silence sad
Trip we after the night's shade;
We the globe can compass soon,
Swifter than the wandering moon.

TITANIA

Come, my lord, and in our flight   100
Tell me how it came this night
That I sleeping here was found,
With these mortals on the ground.

Exeunt. The lovers and BOTTOM *sleep on*

105 *observation*   ritual to mark the dawn of May Day.

106 *vaward*   vanguard or earliest part of the day.

108 *Uncouple*   unleash.

109 *Dispatch*   hurry up.

111–12 *And mark ... conjunction*   they will hear the sound of Theseus's hounds barking, mixed with their own echoes.

113 *Hercules and Cadmus*   two Greek mythological heroes. There is no story in Greek myth to correspond to Hippolyta's tale here.

114 *bayed*   drove to bay, i.e. cornered the bear so it was forced to turn and fight the hounds.

116 *chiding*   angry barking.

120 *kind*   breed.

121 *flewed*   with loosely hanging cheeks, like a bloodhound.
   sanded   with sandy-coloured markings.

123 *Crook-kneed*   with bent rather than straight legs.
   dew-lapped   with folds of skin under their chins.
   Thessalian   from Thessaly in northern Greece.

124 *matched in mouth*   chosen for the musical blend of their barking.

126 *holla*   the cry of the huntsman.

Hunting horns sound. Enter THESEUS, HIPPOLYTA, EGEUS, *and their train.*

THESEUS

    Go one of you, find out the forester,
    For now our observation is performed;   105
    And since we have the vaward of the day,
    My love shall hear the music of my hounds.
    Uncouple in the western valley; let them go;
    Dispatch, I say, and find the forester.

                                     Exit an Attendant

    We will, fair queen, up to the mountain's top,   110
    And mark the musical confusion
    Of hounds and echo in conjunction.

HIPPOLYTA

    I was with Hercules and Cadmus once,
    When in a wood of Crete they bayed the bear
    With hounds of Sparta; never did I hear   115
    Such gallant chiding; for, besides the groves,
    The skies, the fountains, every region near
    Seemed all one mutual cry. I never heard
    So musical a discord, such sweet thunder.

THESEUS

    My hounds are bred out of the Spartan kind,   120
    So flewed, so sanded, and their heads are hung
    With ears that sweep away the morning dew,
    Crook-kneed and dew-lapped, like Thessalian
        bulls;
    Slow in pursuit, but matched in mouth like bells,
    Each under each. A cry more tuneable   125
    Was never holla'd to, nor cheered with horn,
    In Crete, in Sparta, nor in Thessaly.

128 *soft*   wait a moment.

    nymphs   spirits of the forest.

131 *of*   at.

133 *observe*   perform.

134 *our intent*   our wedding plans.

135 *in grace of our solemnity*   in honour of our celebrations.

137 *her choice*   the choice Theseus had offered her in Act 1, to die, join a nunnery or marry Demetrius.

140 *Saint Valentine is past*   it is past St Valentine's Day (February 14th) when birds are supposed to choose their mates. He is the patron saint of lovers.

141 *couple*   form pairs.

145 *jealousy*   suspicion.

146 *by hate*   beside one who hates you.

Judge when you hear. But soft, what nymphs are
  these?

EGEUS

My lord, this is my daughter here asleep,
And this Lysander, this Demetrius is,   130
This Helena, old Nedar's Helena;
I wonder of their being here together.

THESEUS

No doubt they rose up early to observe
The rite of May; and, hearing our intent,
Came here in grace of our solemnity.   135
But speak, Egeus; is not this the day
That Hermia should give answer of her choice?

EGEUS

It is, my lord.

THESEUS

Go bid the huntsmen wake them with their horns.

Horns sound. A shout within. The lovers wake up.

Good morrow, friends! Saint Valentine is past: 140
Begin these wood-birds but to couple now?

LYSANDER

Pardon, my lord.

The lovers kneel.

THESEUS

                    I pray you all, stand up
I know you two are rival enemies.
How comes this gentle concord in the world,
That hatred is so far from jealousy   145
To sleep by hate, and fear no enmity?

147 *amazédly*   in confusion.

151 *do bethink me*   come to think about it.

154 *Without*   out of the reach of.

162 *purpose hither*   plan to come here.

164 *in fancy*   because of her love.

165 *wot*   know.

168 *the remembrance of an idle gaud*   the memory of a useless plaything.

173 *ere*   before.

174 *like in sickness*   like a sick person.

LYSANDER

My lord, I shall reply amazédly,
Half sleep, half waking. But as yet, I swear,
I cannot truly say how I came here.
But as I think, for truly would I speak,   150
And now I do bethink me, so it is:
I came with Hermia hither: our intent
Was to be gone from Athens, where we might,
Without the peril of the Athenian law –

EGEUS

Enough, enough, my lord; you have enough;   155
I beg the law, the law, upon his head.
They would have stolen away; they would,
      Demetrius,
Thereby to have defeated you and me:
You of your wife, and me of my consent;
Of my consent, that she should be your wife.   160

DEMETRIUS

My lord, fair Helen told me of their stealth,
Of this their purpose hither to this wood,
And I in fury hither followed them;
Fair Helena in fancy following me.
But, my good lord, I wot not by what power,   165
But by some power it is, my love to Hermia,
Melted as doth the snow, seems to me now
As the remembrance of an idle gaud,
Which in my childhood I did dote upon;
And all the faith, the virtue of my heart,   170
The object and the pleasure of mine eye,
Is only Helena. To her, my lord,
Was I betrothed ere I saw Hermia;
But like in sickness did I loathe this food;

175 *come to* restored it.

179 *discourse* topic of conversation.

180 *overbear* overrule.

183 *something worn* somewhat advanced (it is no longer early enough to hunt).

184 *purposed* proposed.

185 *three and three* three men and three women.

190 *parted eye* double vision.

195 *yet* still.

But, as in health, come to my natural taste,   175
Now I do wish it, love it, long for it,
And will for evermore be true to it.

THESEUS

Fair lovers, you are fortunately met;
Of this discourse we more will hear anon.
Egeus, I will overbear your will,   180
For in the temple, by and by, with us
These couples shall eternally be knit.
And, for the morning now is something worn,
Our purposed hunting shall be set aside.
Away with us to Athens; three and three,   185
We'll hold a feast in great solemnity.
Come, Hippolyta.

Exeunt all but the lovers and BOTTOM, *still asleep*

DEMETRIUS

These things seem small and undistinguishable,
Like far-off mountains turnéd into clouds.

HERMIA

Methinks I see these things with parted eye,   190
When every thing seems double.

HELENA

                              So methinks;
And I have found Demetrius, like a jewel,
Mine own, and not mine own.

DEMETRIUS

                              Are you sure
That we are awake? It seems to me
That yet we sleep, we dream. Do not you think   195
The Duke was here, and bid us follow him?

201 *my cue*   Bottom still thinks he is at the rehearsal.

204 *Stolen hence*   crept away from here.

208 *expound*   explain.

210–11 *patched fool*   jester in patched clothing.

212–15 *The eye ... dream was*   a garbled version of some words of St Paul
(I Corinthians, 2:9) 'Eye hath not seen nor ear heard, nor hath the heart of man
conceived what things God has prepared for those that love him'. Bottom wants
to convey that he has been in heaven.

217 *no bottom*   no rational explanation.

219 *Peradventure*   perhaps.

220 *her death*   the death of Thisby in the play.

HERMIA

Yea, and my father.

HELENA

And Hippolyta.

LYSANDER

And he did bid us follow to the temple.

DEMETRIUS

Why then, we are awake; let's follow him,
And by the way let us recount our dreams.   200

Exeunt the lovers

BOTTOM (*waking up*)

When my cue comes, call me, and I will answer.
My next is 'Most fair Pyramus'. Heigh-ho! Peter
Quince! Flute the bellows-mender! Snout the
tinker! Starveling! God's my life! Stolen hence,
and left me asleep! I have had a most rare vision. 205
I have had a dream, past the wit of man to say
what dream it was. Man is but an ass if he go
about to expound this dream. Methought I was
– there is no man can tell what. Methought I was,
and methought I had – but man is but a patched 210
fool, if he will offer to say what methought I had.
The eye of man hath not heard, the ear of man
hath not seen, man's hand is not able to taste, his
tongue to conceive, nor his heart to report, what
my dream was. I will get Peter Quince to write a 215
ballad of this dream; it shall be called 'Bottom's
Dream', because it hath no bottom; and I will sing
it in the latter end of a play, before the Duke.
Peradventure, to make it the more gracious, I shall
sing it at her death.   220

Exit

3 *He cannot be heard of*   no one has seen him.
  Out of doubt   certainly, without doubt.

4 *transported*   carried away, kidnapped.

5 *marred*   spoiled.

5–6 *It goes not forward*   it cannot go on.

8 *discharge*   take the role of.

11 *the best person*   most suitable in appearance.

12 *paramour*   lover.

13 *paragon*   model of excellence.

14 *thing of naught*   a shameful thing.

Scene two

Athens.

Enter QUINCE, FLUTE, SNOUT, *and* STARVELING.

QUINCE

Have you sent to Bottom's house? Is he come
home yet?

STARVELING

He cannot be heard of. Out of doubt he is
transported.

FLUTE

If he come not, then the play is marred. It goes   5
not forward, doth it?

QUINCE

It is not possible: you have not a man in all Athens
able to discharge Pyramus, but he.

FLUTE

No; he hath simply the best wit of any handicraft
man in Athens.   10

QUINCE

Yea, and the best person too; and he is a very
paramour for a sweet voice.

FLUTE

You must say 'paragon'. A paramour is, God bless
us, a thing of naught.

Enter SNUG.

SNUG

Masters! the Duke is coming from the temple, and 15
there is two or three lords and ladies more

163

17 *If our sport had gone forward*   if our play had been ready to perform.

18 *made men*   men who had secured their fortunes.

19–24 *sixpence a day ... or nothing*   Flute is suggesting that Bottom would have made such an impression in the role of Pyramus that the Duke would have given him a pension for life of sixpence a day, comfortably more than the average wage for a working man in Elizabethan England.

20 *scaped*   failed to be given.

21 *An*   if.

25 *hearts*   grand-hearted fellows.

26 *courageous*   Quince means brave in its Elizabethan sense of splendid.

30 *right as it fell out*   exactly as it happened.

32 *of me*   about me.

33 *apparel*   costumes for the play.

34 *strings to your beards*   strings to tie on false beards.

35 *pumps*   dancing shoes.

35 *presently*   straight away.

37 *preferred*   put on the list of entertainments which the Duke will choose from.

38 *pare*   trim.

married. If our sport had gone forward, we had all
been made men.

FLUTE

O sweet bully Bottom! Thus hath he lost sixpence
a day during his life; he could not have scaped   20
sixpence a day. An the Duke had not given him
sixpence a day for playing Pyramus, I'll be
hanged. He would have deserved it: Sixpence a
day in Pyramus, or nothing.

Enter BOTTOM.

BOTTOM

Where are these lads? Where are these hearts?   25

QUINCE

Bottom! O, most courageous day! O, most happy
hour!

BOTTOM

Masters, I am to discourse wonders; but ask me
not what, for if I tell you, I am no true Athenian.
I will tell you everything right as it fell out.   30

QUINCE

Let us hear, sweet Bottom.

BOTTOM

Not a word of me: all that I will tell you is, that
the Duke hath dined. Get your apparel together,
good strings to your beards, new ribbons to your
pumps, meet presently at the palace; every man   35
look o'er his part; for the short and the long is, our
play is preferred. In any case, let Thisby have
clean linen: and let not him that plays the lion pare

41 *sweet breath*   sweet words, which must not be spoiled by breath smelling of onions or garlic.

his nails, for they shall hang out for the lion's
claws. And, most dear actors, eat no onions, nor 40
garlic; for we are to utter sweet breath, and I do
not doubt but to hear them say, it is a sweet
comedy. No more words: away, go away!

Exeunt

The workmen perform their play: Stratford-upon-Avon Royal Shakespeare Company production of A Midsummer Night's Dream, 1984.

168

Act 5: summary

Theseus and Hippolyta discuss the strange events of the night, and how it all seems to have turned out for the best. They are joined by the other newly-weds, Hermia and Lysander, and Helena and Demetrius. They are offered a selection of entertainments for the evening, and Theseus chooses 'Pyramus and Thisby', despite the dreadful review given to it by his entertainments manager, Philostrate.

The play is performed, not without mishaps, and the nobles have fun at the expense of the ham acting, especially Bottom's, and the would-be impressive language of the play. Nevertheless, the dramas and misunderstandings of the story remind us of the ordeal the lovers have so recently suffered in the wood. The play is successfully concluded with the dramatic death of Bottom as Pyramus and Flute as Thisby, and Theseus thanks the actors graciously for their efforts. The entertainments end with Bottom and his friends performing a dance for the nobles. Midnight strikes, and the newly-wedded couples go off to bed.

Puck enters, followed by Oberon, Titania and the rest of the fairies. They have come to sing and dance, and to bless the house and the marriage beds of the newly-married couples. They depart, leaving Puck behind.

Puck, or rather the actor playing Puck, then speaks directly to the audience. He hopes the audience enjoyed the play, and if they did not, promises that the company will do better in future. He wishes them goodnight, and asks for their applause.

1 *that* that which.

3 *antique fables* ancient stories.

toys foolish, idle stories.

4 *seething* over-active.

5 *shaping fantasies* creative imaginations.

apprehend conjures up.

6 *comprehends* understands.

8 *all compact* entirely made up of.

11 *Helen* Helen of Troy, a woman of legendary beauty over whom the Trojan War was fought.

brow of Egypt the face of any gypsy woman.

14 *bodies forth* gives shape to, as clear mental pictures.

17 *local habitation* a particular place to live.

19 *apprehend* see note to line 5 above.

20 *It comprehends ... that joy* it comprises or includes an imagined bringer of that joy.

Act Five

Scene one

Athens.

Enter THESEUS, HIPPOLYTA, PHILOSTRATE *and Attendants.*

HIPPOLYTA

'T is strange, my Theseus, that these lovers speak
   of.

THESEUS

More strange than true. I never may believe
These antique fables nor these fairy toys.
Lovers and madmen have such seething brains,
Such shaping fantasies, that apprehend   5
More than cool reason ever comprehends.
The lunatic, the lover, and the poet
Are of imagination all compact.
One sees more devils than vast hell can hold;
That is the madman. The lover, all as frantic,   10
Sees Helen's beauty in a brow of Egypt.
The poet's eye, in a fine frenzy rolling,
Doth glance from heaven to earth, from earth to
   heaven,
And as imagination bodies forth
The forms of things unknown, the poet's pen   15
Turns them to shapes, and gives to airy nothing
A local habitation and a name.
Such tricks hath strong imagination
That, if it would but apprehend some joy,
It comprehends some bringer of that joy.   20
Or in the night, imagining some fear,
How easy is a bush supposed a bear.

23–6 *But all ... great constancy*   but when we consider all the events of the night, with all the lovers' minds affected in the same way ('transfigured so together'), we can see that there is more to it than imagination ('fancy's images'), and that it is in fact all very consistent and reliable.

27 *howsoever*   in any case.

admirable   to be wondered at.

30 *More*   more joy.

32 *masques*   entertainments with drama, music and dancing.

35 *manager of mirth*   organiser of entertainments.

36 *revels*   entertainments.

39 *abridgement*   way of passing the time.

40 *beguile*   charm away.

HIPPOLYTA

But all the story of the night told over,
And all their minds transfigured so together,
More witnesseth than fancy's images,   25
And grows to something of great constancy;
But howsoever, strange and admirable.

Enter LYSANDER, DEMETRIUS, HERMIA *and* HELENA.

THESEUS

Here come the lovers, full of joy and mirth:
Joy, gentle friends, joy and fresh days of love
Accompany your hearts!

LYSANDER

                More than to us,   30
Wait in your royal walks, your board, your bed!

THESEUS

Come now, what masques, what dances shall we
    have
To wear away this long age of three hours
Between our after-supper, and bed-time?
Where is our usual manager of mirth?   35
What revels are in hand? Is there no play
To ease the anguish of a torturing hour?
Call Philostrate.

PHILOSTRATE

                Here, mighty Theseus.

THESEUS

Say, what abridgement have you for this evening?
What masque? What music? How shall we beguile 40
The lazy time, if not with some delight?

42 *brief*   list.

sports   entertainments.

ripe   ready.

44 *Centaurs*   mythical beasts, with a man's head, arms and torso and a horse's body and legs.

45 *eunuch*   castrated man with a high voice.

46 *my love*   Hippolyta.

47 *In glory of my kinsman Hercules*   in praise of Hercules. He and Theseus were cousins.

48 *tipsy Bacchanals*   Bacchus was the god of wine, and his followers, the Bacchanals, celebrated him by getting drunk.

49 *Thracian singer*   in Greek mythology, Orpheus, who was from Thrace (hence 'Thracian') was attacked by drunken followers of Bacchus.

50 *device*   play.

52 *thrice three Muses*   in Greek mythology there were nine Muses who inspired the Arts.

53 *late*   lately.

55 *sorting with*   suitable for.

60 *concord*   harmony.

65 *fitted*   suitable for his part.

PHILOSTRATE

There is a brief how many sports are ripe:
Make choice of which your Highness will see first.

THESEUS (*reads*)

'The battle with the Centaurs, to be sung
By an Athenian eunuch, to the harp'.   45
We'll none of that. That have I told my love
In glory of my kinsman Hercules.
'The riot of the tipsy Bacchanals,
Tearing the Thracian singer in their rage'.
That is an old device, and it was played   50
When I from Thebes came last a conqueror.
'The thrice three Muses, mourning for the death
Of Learning, late deceased in beggary'.
That is some satire, keen and critical,
Not sorting with a nuptial ceremony.   55
'A tedious brief scene of young Pyramus
And his love Thisby; very tragical mirth'.
Merry and tragical? Tedious, and brief?
That is, hot ice, and wondrous strange snow.
How shall we find the concord of this discord?   60

PHILOSTRATE

A play there is, my lord, some ten words long,
Which is as brief as I have known a play;
But by ten words, my lord, it is too long,
Which makes it tedious; for in all the play
There is not one word apt, one player fitted.   65
And tragical, my noble lord, it is;
For Pyramus therein doth kill himself.
Which when I saw rehearsed, I must confess,
Made mine eyes water; but more merry tears,
The passion of loud laughter never shed.   70

72 *Hard-handed men*   men who work with their hands.

73 *laboured in their minds*   worked with their brains.

74 *unbreathed*   unpractised.

75 *against*   in preparation for.

79 *sport*   entertainment, fun.

intents   intentions.

80 *Extremely stretched*   much more than they can manage.

conned   learned (the lines).

83 *simpleness*   innocence.

tender   offer.

85 *wretchedness*   weakness, lack of ability.

o'ercharged   overburdened.

86 *And duty ... perishing*   someone failing by trying to achieve more than they are capable of.

88 *in this kind*   of this sort (i.e. acting in a play).

THESEUS

What are they that do play it?

PHILOSTRATE

Hard-handed men, that work in Athens here,
Which never laboured in their minds till now;
And now have toiled their unbreathed memories
With this same play, against your nuptial.   75

THESEUS

And we will hear it.

PHILOSTRATE

No, my noble lord,
It is not for you. I have heard it over,
And it is nothing, nothing in the world;
Unless you can find sport in their intents,
Extremely stretched and conned with cruel pain,   80
To do you service.

THESEUS

I will hear that play.
For never any thing can be amiss
When simpleness and duty tender it.
Go, bring them in; and take your places, ladies.

Exit PHILOSTRATE

HIPPOLYTA

I love not to see wretchedness o'ercharged,   85
And duty in his service perishing.

THESEUS

Why, gentle sweet, you shall see no such thing.

HIPPOLYTA

He says they can do nothing in this kind.

90 *Our sport ... mistake*   our fun will come from watching them making mistakes.

91–2 *noble respect ... not merit*   we will show consideration for what they intend (what 'might' have been) rather than what they actually achieve.

93 *clerks*   scholars.

94 *premeditated*   well rehearsed.

96 *periods*   full stops.

97 *throttle their practised accents*   choke on their prepared speeches.

101 *modesty*   embarrassment.

fearful duty   duty which caused them to be nervous.

102 *rattling*   noisy and unhesitating.

103 *saucy*   cheeky.

audacious   bold.

105 *to my capacity*   to the best of my understanding.

106 *addressed*   ready to start.

108–17 Peter Quince is very nervous, and his speech does not make much sense because he makes 'periods' (full stops) 'in the midst of sentences' as Theseus has just described. It is possible to make sense of it by repunctuating it.

108 *will*   intention.

112 *in despite*   to annoy you.

113 *minding*   meaning, having in mind to.

THESEUS

The kinder we, to give them thanks for nothing.
Our sport shall be to take what they mistake;   90
And what poor duty cannot do, noble respect
Takes it in might, not merit.
Where I have come, great clerks have puposéd
To greet me with premeditated welcomes;
Where I have seen them shiver and look pale,   95
Make periods in the midst of sentences,
Throttle their practised accent in their fears,
And in conclusion, dumbly have broken off,
Not paying me a welcome. Trust me, sweet,
Out of this silence yet I picked a welcome;   100
And in the modesty of fearful duty
I read as much as from the rattling tongue
Of saucy and audacious eloquence.
Love, therefore, and tongue-tied simplicity,
In least speak most, to my capacity.   105

Re-enter PHILOSTRATE.

PHILOSTRATE

So please your Grace, the Prologue is addressed.

THESEUS

Let him approach.

Trumpets sound. Enter QUINCE *as the* PROLOGUE.

QUINCE (*as* PROLOGUE)

If we offend, it is with our good will.
That you should think, we come not to offend,
But with good will. To show our simple skill,   110
That is the true beginning of our end.
Consider then, we come but in despite.
We do not come, as minding to content you,

179

118 *doth not stand upon points*   does not pay attention to punctuation.

119 *rid*   ridden.

120 *stop*   full stop.

121 *true*   properly.

123 *in government*   in control.

125 *impaired*   damaged.

126 *Gentles*   ladies and gentlemen.

perchance   perhaps.

131 *sunder*   separate.

Our true intent is. All for your delight,
We are not here. That you should here repent you, 115
The actors are at hand: and by their show,
You shall know all, that you are like to know.

THESEUS
This fellow doth not stand upon points.

LYSANDER
He hath rid his prologue like a rough colt: he
knows not the stop. A good moral, my lord: it is 120
not enough to speak, but to speak true.

HIPPOLYTA
Indeed he hath played on his prologue like a child
on a recorder, a sound, but not in government.

THESEUS
His speech was like a tangled chain: nothing
impaired, but all disordered. Who is next?   125

A trumpet sounds. Enter PYRAMUS (BOTTOM), THISBE (FLUTE),
WALL (SNOUT), MOONSHINE (STARVELING), *and* LION
(SNUG), *who stand in line while* QUINCE *speaks as* PROLOGUE.

QUINCE (*as* PROLOGUE)
Gentles, perchance you wonder at this show;
But wonder on, till truth make all things plain.
This man is Pyramus, if you would know;
This beauteous lady Thisby is certain.
This man with lime and rough-cast doth present 130
Wall, that vile Wall, which did these lovers sunder:
And through Wall's chink, poor souls, they are
    content
To whisper: at the which, let no man wonder.
This man, with lantern, dog, and bush of thorn,
Presenteth Moonshine; for, if you will know,   135

181

136 *think no scorn*   did not think it shameful.

138 *hight*   is called.

141 *mantle*   scarf.

   fall   drop.

143 *tall*   handsome.

146 *broached*   pierced.

147 *tarrying*   waiting.

150 *At large discourse*   speak at full length.

153 *interlude*   play.

154 *present*   represent.

By moonshine did these lovers think no scorn
To meet at Ninus' tomb, there, there to woo.
This grisly beast, which Lion hight by name,
The trusty Thisby, coming first by night,
Did scare away, or rather did affright: 140
And as she fled, her mantle she did fall;
Which Lion vile with bloody mouth did stain.
Anon comes Pyramus, sweet youth and tall,
And finds his trusty Thisby's mantle slain;
Whereat with blade, with bloody blameful blade,   145
He bravely broached his boiling bloody breast,
And Thisby, tarrying in mulberry shade,
His dagger drew, and died. For all the rest,
Let Lion, Moonshine, Wall, and Lovers twain,
At large discourse, while here they do remain.   150

Exeunt all the players but SNOUT (WALL)

THESEUS

I wonder if the lion be to speak.

DEMETRIUS

No wonder, my lord: one lion may, when many
   asses do.

SNOUT (*as* WALL)

In this same interlude it doth befall
That I, one Snout by name, present a wall:
And such a wall, as I would have you think,   155
That had in it a crannied hole or chink,
Through which the lovers, Pyramus and Thisby,
Did whisper often, very secretly.
This loam, this rough-cast, and this stone doth
   show
That I am that same Wall; the truth is so.   160

161 *right and sinister* right and left.
164 *wittiest partition* most intelligent wall.
174 *eyne* eyes.
175 *Jove shield you* may God protect you.
179 *being sensible* having feelings.
     curse again say something in reply.

And this the cranny is, right and sinister,
Through which the fearful lovers are to whisper.

THESEUS

Would you desire lime and hair to speak better?

DEMETRIUS

It is the wittiest partition that ever I heard
discourse, my lord.   165

THESEUS

Pyramus draws near the Wall; silence.

Enter BOTTOM *as* PYRAMUS.

BOTTOM (*as* PYRAMUS)
    O grim-looked night, O night with hue so black!
    O night, which ever art when day is not!
    O night, O night; alack, alack, alack,
    I fear my Thisby's promise is forgot.   170
    And thou O wall, O sweet, O lovely wall,
    That stand'st between her father's ground and
        mine,
    Thou wall, O wall, O sweet and lovely wall,
    Show me thy chink, to blink through with mine
        eyne.

SNOUT *holds up his fingers.*

    Thanks, courteous wall: Jove shield thee well for
        this!   175
    But what see I? No Thisby do I see.
    O wicked wall, through whom I see no bliss,
    Cursed be thy stones for thus deceiving me!

THESEUS

The wall, methinks, being sensible, should curse
    again.

185

180–3 *No, in truth ... comes*   Bottom addresses these words to Theseus.

182 *fall pat*   turn out exactly.

189 *an*   if.

193 *Limander*   a mistake for Leander, a mythical Greek hero who drowned when trying to swim to his love, Hero.

194 *Helen*   Flute's mistake for Hero.

Fates   the three sisters, who in Greek mythology, ruled the destinies of us all.

195 *Shafalus to Procrus*   another mistaken reference, this time to Cephalus, who was renowned in Greek mythology for his devotion to his wife Procris.

BOTTOM

No, in truth sir, he should not. 'Deceiving me' is 180
Thisby's cue; she is to enter now, and I am to spy
her through the wall. You shall see it will fall pat
as I told you: yonder she comes.

Enter FLUTE (*as* THISBE).

FLUTE (*as* THISBE)

O wall, full often hast thou heard my moans,
For parting my fair Pyramus and me. 185
My cherry lips have often kissed thy stones;
Thy stones, with lime and hair knit up in thee.

BOTTOM (*as* PYRAMUS)

I see a voice; now will I to the chink,
To spy an I can hear my Thisby's face.
Thisby! 190

FLUTE (*as* THISBE)

My love! thou art my love, I think.

BOTTOM (*as* PYRAMUS)

Think what thou wilt, I am thy lover's grace,
And like Limander am I trusty still.

FLUTE (*as* THISBE)

And I like Helen, till the Fates me kill.

BOTTOM (*as* PYRAMUS)

Not Shafalus to Procrus was so true. 195

FLUTE (*as* THISBE)

As Shafalus to Procrus, I to you.

BOTTOM (*as* PYRAMUS)

O kiss me through the hole of this vile wall.

199 *Ninny's tomb* Bottom persists in mistaking Ninny for Ninus, despite Quince's attempts to put him right in the rehearsal (see page 86, note to line 96).

200 *'Tide ... death* whether I live or die.

201 *dischargéd* performed.

203 *mural* wall.

204 *No remedy* it cannot be helped.

207 *The best in this kind* the best actors.

  but only.

208 *imagination amend them* if our imaginations make up for their shortcomings.

FLUTE (*as* THISBE)

I kiss the wall's hole, not your lips at all.

BOTTOM (*as* PYRAMUS)

Wilt thou at Ninny's tomb meet me straightway?

FLUTE (*as* THISBE)

'Tide life, 'tide death, I come without delay.　　200

Exeunt BOTTOM *and* FLUTE

SNOUT (*as* WALL)

Thus have I, Wall, my part dischargéd so;
And being done, thus Wall away doth go.

Exit

THESEUS

Now is the mural down between the two neighbours.

DEMETRIUS

No remedy, my lord, when walls are so wilful, to
hear without warning.　　205

HIPPOLYTA

This is the silliest stuff that ever I heard.

THESEUS

The best in this kind are but shadows, and the
worst are no worse, if imagination amend them.

HIPPOLYTA

It must be your imagination then, and not theirs.

THESEUS

If we imagine no worse of them than they of them-210
selves, they may pass for excellent men. Here come
two noble beasts in, a man and a lion.

215 *perchance*   perhaps.

218 *fell*   fierce.

   dam   mother. Snug does not want to be mistaken for a female lion.

219 *in strife*   in an aggressive manner.

220 *'t were pity on my life*   I should have to plead for my life (because I should
   have done something deserving of punishment).

221 *gentle*   polite.

   conscience   sensitivity.

223 *very*   real.

   fox   foxes were regarded as cunning rather than brave.

224 *goose*   geese, on the other hand, are neither brave nor cunning, but simply
   stupid.

230 *lanthorn*   lantern.

   hornéd   crescent.

Enter SNUG *as* LION *and* STARVELING *as* MOONSHINE.

SNUG (*as* LION)

You, ladies, you, whose gentle hearts do fear
The smallest monstrous mouse that creeps on
    floor,
May now, perchance, both quake and tremble here 215
When Lion rough in wildest rage doth roar.
Then know that I, one Snug the joiner, am
A lion fell, nor else no lion's dam:
For if I should as Lion come in strife
Into this place, 't were pity on my life.   220

THESEUS

A very gentle beast, and of a good conscience.

DEMETRIUS

The very best at a beast, my lord, that e'er I saw.

LYSANDER

This Lion is a very fox for his valour.

THESEUS

True, and a goose for his discretion.

DEMETRIUS

Not so, my lord; for his valour cannot carry his 225
discretion, and the fox carries the goose.

THESEUS

His discretion, I am sure, cannot carry his valour;
for the goose carries not the fox. It is well; leave
it to his discretion, and let us listen to the Moon.

STARVELING (*as* MOONSHINE)

This lanthorn doth the hornéd moon present.   230

231 *He should ... head*   horns were the sign of a man whose wife had been unfaithful.

232–3 *He is ... circumference*   he is a full moon, not a crescent, so you cannot see his 'horns'.

235 *Man i' th' Moon*   the marks on the surface of the moon can be interpreted as the features of a face.

240 *in snuff*   of candles, in need of having the wick trimmed, but 'in snuff' also meant angry when used of people.

245 *stay the time*   wait for the right moment.

DEMETRIUS

He should have worn the horns on his head.

THESEUS

He is no crescent and his horns are invisible,
within the circumference.

STARVELING (*as* MOONSHINE)

This lanthorn doth the hornéd moon present:
Myself the Man i' th' Moon do seem to be.   235

THESEUS

This is the greatest error of all the rest; the man
should be put into the lantern. How is it else the
Man i' th' Moon?

DEMETRIUS

He dares not come there for the candle; for you
see, it is already in snuff.   240

HIPPOLYTA

I am a-weary of this Moon; would he would
change!

THESEUS

It appears, by his small light of discretion, that he
is in the wane: but yet, in courtesy, in all reason,
we must stay the time.   245

LYSANDER

Proceed, Moon.

STARVELING (*as* MOONSHINE)

All that I have to say is to tell you that the
lanthorn is the Moon; I, the Man i' th' Moon; this
thorn-bush, my thorn-bush; and this dog, my dog.

259 *moused*   the lion has Thisby's mantle in his mouth like a cat with a mouse.

DEMETRIUS
Why, all these should be in the lantern: for all 250
these are in the Moon. But silence, here comes
Thisby.

Re-enter FLUTE (*as* THISBE).

FLUTE (*as* THISBE)
This is old Ninny's tomb. Where is my love?

SNUG (*as* LION) *roars*
Oh-h-h-!

THISBE *runs off.*

DEMETRIUS
Well roared, Lion.   255

THESEUS
Well run, Thisby.

HIPPOLYTA
Well shone, Moon.
Truly, the Moon shines with a good grace.

SNUG (*as* LION) *tears* THISBE's *mantle, and exit.*

THESEUS
Well moused, Lion.

Re-enter BOTTOM (*as* PYRAMUS).

DEMETRIUS
And then came Pyramus.   260

LYSANDER
And so the Lion vanished.

BOTTOM (*as* PYRAMUS)
Sweet Moon, I thank thee for thy sunny beams;

268 *dole* sorrow.

274 *Furies* fierce creatures in Greek mythology who hounded and savaged murderers.

fell foul.

275 *Fates* see page 30, note to line 34.

276 *Cut thread and thrum* the Fates wove a thread for each person's life, and when it was cut, the person died.

280 *Beshrew* curse.

281 *frame* create.

282 *deflowered* ravished.

288 *pap* breast.

290 *hop* beat.

I thank thee, Moon, for shining now so bright;
For by thy gracious, golden, glittering gleams,
I trust to take of truest Thisby sight.   265
But stay! O spite!
But mark, poor knight,
What dreadful dole is here!
Eyes, do you see?
How can it be?   270
O dainty duck! O dear!
Thy mantle good,
What, stained with blood?
Approach, ye Furies fell:
O Fates! come, come: 275
Cut thread and thrum,
Quail, crush, conclude, and quell!

THESEUS

This passion, and the death of a dear friend, would
go near to make a man look sad.

HIPPOLYTA

Beshrew my heart, but I pity the man.   280

BOTTOM (*as* PYRAMUS)

O wherefore, Nature, didst thou lions frame?
Since lion vile hath here deflowered my dear:
Which is – no, no, which was – the fairest Dame
That lived, that loved, that liked, that looked with
      cheer.   285
Come tears, confound:
Out sword, and wound
The pap of Pyramus:
Ay, that left pap,
Where heart doth hop;   290
Thus die I, thus, thus, thus.

197

298 *die*   one of a pair of dice.

    ace   the side of the die with one spot on it.

306 *passion*   suffering.

309 *mote*   speck of dust.

309–10 *which Pyramus, which Thisby*   whether Pyramus or Thisby.

Stabs himself.

Now am I dead,
Now am I fled,
My soul is in the sky,
Tongue, lose thy light,   295
Moon, take thy flight,

Exit STARVELING *as* MOONSHINE

Now die, die, die, die, die. (*'Dies'*)

DEMETRIUS

No die, but an ace for him; for he is but one.

LYSANDER

Less than an ace, man; for he is dead, he is
nothing.   300

THESEUS

With the help of a surgeon he might yet recover,
and prove an ass.

HIPPOLYTA

How chance Moonshine is gone before Thisby
comes back, and finds her lover?

Re-enter FLUTE (*as* THISBE).

THESEUS

She will find him by starlight. Here she comes, and 305
her passion ends the play.

HIPPOLYTA

Methinks she should not use a long one for such
a Pyramus; I hope she will be brief.

DEMETRIUS

A mote will turn the balance, which Pyramus,

199

311 *warrant* preserve.

313 *videlicet* (Latin) namely or thus, now abbreviated to *viz.*

326 *Sisters Three* the Fates; see page 30, note to line 34 and page 196, note to line 275.

329 *gore* blood.

330 *shore* cut.

334 *imbrue* soak with blood.

which Thisby is the better; he for a man, God 310
warrant us, she for a woman, God bless us.

LYSANDER

She hath spied him already with those sweet eyes.

DEMETRIUS

And she moans, *videlicet*:

FLUTE (*as* THISBE)

Asleep, my love?
What, dead, my dove? 315
O Pyramus, arise!
Speak, speak. Quite dumb?
Dead, dead? A tomb
Must cover thy sweet eyes.
These lily lips, 320
This cherry nose,
These yellow cowslip cheeks,
Are gone, are gone:
Lovers, make moan:
His eyes were green as leeks. 325
O Sisters Three,
Come, come to me,
With hands as pale as milk;
Lay them in gore,
Since you have shore 330
With shears his thread of silk.
Tongue, not a word:
Come, trusty sword:
Come blade, my breast imbrue:

Stabs herself.

And farewell, friends; 335
Thus Thisby ends;
Adieu, adieu, adieu. ('*Dies*')

342 *Bergomask*   country dance from Bergamo in Italy.

346 *Marry*   by the Virgin Mary, a mild swear word.

347 *writ*   wrote.

352 *iron tongue*   the iron clapper of the bell.

354 *out-sleep*   oversleep.

355 *overwatched*   stayed up too late.

356 *palpable gross*   obviously crude.

     beguiled   charmed away.

357 *heavy gait of night*   the slow pace of night.

358 *solemnity*   celebration.

359 *nightly revels*   entertainments every night.

THESEUS

Moonshine and Lion are left to bury the dead.

DEMETRIUS

Ay, and Wall too.

BOTTOM (*getting up*)

No, I assure you, the wall is down that parted their 340
fathers. Will it please you to see the epilogue, or
to hear a Bergomask dance between two of our
company?

THESEUS

No epilogue, I pray you; for your play needs no
excuse. Never excuse; for when the players are all 345
dead there need none to be blamed. Marry, if he
that writ it had played Pyramus, and hanged
himself in Thisby's garter, it would have been a
fine tragedy: and so it is truly, and very notably
discharged. But come, your Bergomask: let your 350
epilogue alone.

A Bergomask dance

The iron tongue of midnight hath told twelve.
Lovers, to bed; 't is almost fairy time.
I fear we shall out-sleep the coming morn
As much as we this night have overwatched.   355
This palpable gross play hath well beguiled
The heavy gait of night. Sweet friends, to bed.
A fortnight hold we this solemnity,
In nightly revels and new jollity.

Exeunt all

Enter PUCK *with a broom.*

361 *behowls*   howls at.

363 *fordone*   worn out.

364 *wasted brands*   burnt-out logs on the fire.

366–7 *Puts the ... shroud*   reminds the sick person in bed of the sheet ('shroud') that their body will be wrapped in. Owls were associated with death.

370 *sprite*   spirit of the person buried there.

373 *triple Hecate*   goddess of darkness and magic, who had a three-in-one identity.

376 *frolic*   playful and frisky.

380 *glimmering*   flickering.

382 *sprite*   spirit.

384 *ditty*   song.

385 *trippingly*   nimbly and lightly.

386 *rehearse ... rote*   repeat your song from memory.

PUCK

Now the hungry lion roars, 360
And the wolf behowls the moon;
Whilst the heavy ploughman snores,
All with weary task fordone.
Now the wasted brands do glow,
Whilst the screech-owl, screeching loud, 365
Puts the wretch that lies in woe
In remembrance of a shroud.
Now it is the time of night
That the graves, all gaping wide,
Every one lets forth his sprite, 370
In the church-way paths to glide.
And we fairies, that do run
By the triple Hecate's team
From the presence of the sun,
Following darkness like a dream, 375
Now are frolic; not a mouse
Shall disturb this hallowed house.
I am sent with broom before,
To sweep the dust behind the door.

Enter OBERON *and* TITANIA, *the King and Queen of Fairies,
with their train, bearing lighted candles.*

OBERON

Through the house give glimmering light, 380
By the dead and drowsy fire;
Every elf and fairy sprite
Hop as light as bird from brier;
And this ditty after me
Sing, and dance it trippingly. 385

TITANIA

First rehearse your song by rote,

205

391 *stray* wander.

394 *issue* children.

create conceived.

395 *fortunate* lucky.

398 *blots of Nature's hand* natural defects.

399 *stand* occur.

401 *mark prodigious* ominous or unlucky birthmark.

402 *Despiséd in nativity* feared and hated at a child's birth.

404 *consecrate* sacred, consecrated.

405 *take his gait* make his way.

406 *several* separate.

410 *make no stay* do not wait.

412 *shadows* this means both fairies and actors. Theseus calls actors 'shadows' in line 207.

To each word a warbling note.
Hand in hand, with fairy grace,
Will we sing and bless this place.

OBERON *leads, and the Fairies sing and dance.*

OBERON

Now until the break of day,   390
Through this house each fairy stray.
To the best bride-bed will we,
Which by us shall blessèd be;
And the issue there create
Ever shall be fortunate.   395
So shall all the couples three
Ever true in loving be;
And the blots of Nature's hand
Shall not in their issue stand.
Never mole, hare-lip, nor scar,   400
Nor mark prodigious, such as are
Despisèd in nativity,
Shall upon their children be.
With this field-dew consecrate,
Every fairy take his gait,   405
And each several chamber bless,
Through this palace, with sweet peace;
And the owner of it blest
Ever shall in safety rest.
Trip away, make no stay;   410
Meet me all by break of day.

Exeunt, OBERON *and* TITANIA *behind, the Fairies*
through the house. PUCK *stays*

PUCK

If we shadows have offended,
Think but this, and all is mended,

417 *No more yielding*   offering no more.

418 *Gentles*   see page 180, note to line 126.

   reprehend   criticise.

419 *mend*   improve.

421 *unearnéd luck*   more luck then we deserve.

422 *'scape*   escape.

   serpent's tongue   hissing made by a disapproving audience.

426 *Give me your hands*   applaud.

427 *restore amends*   make improvements in return.

That you have but slumbered here,
While these visions did appear. 415
And this weak and idle theme,
No more yielding but a dream,
Gentles, do not reprehend:
If you pardon, we will mend.
And, as I am an honest Puck, 420
If we have unearnéd luck
Now to scape the serpent's tongue,
We will make amends ere long,
Else the Puck a liar call.
So, good night unto you all. 425
Give me your hands, if we be friends,
And Robin shall restore amends.

Exit

Study programme

Before reading the play

Plot

In order to get an overall idea of the story of the play, read the summaries at the beginning of each act. Then, to check that you are clear about what you have read, complete the following two assignments.

1. Retell the story of the play in a group, each person offering one line at a time.

2. Fill in the following chart, showing which character is coupled with which at different stages in the play: ⟶ = loves ⋙ = quarrelling

WHEN	WHO	
Before the play starts	Lysander ⇄	*Hermia*
	Demetrius ⇄	*Helena*
During Act 1	Theseus ⇄	*Hippolyta*
	Lysander ⇄	*Hermia*
	Helena ⟶	*Demethrius* ↑
At the start of Act 2	Oberon ⋙	*Titania*
After the first application of love juice to Lysander's eyes	Lysander ⟶	*Helena*
	Hermia ↑ ⟵	*Demethrius* ↑
After Oberon has applied love juice to Demetrius' eyes	Lysander ⟶	*Helena*
	Hermia	*Demethrius* ↑↑
	Titania ⟶	*Bottom* (w/ ass' head)

211

After Puck releases Titania from the spell	Titania ⇌	*Oberon*
After Puck crushes a herb into Lysander's eye	Lysander ⇌	*Hermia*
	Demetrius ⇌	*Helena*
During the wedding celebrations	Hippolyta ⇌	*Theseus*

Themes

☐ *A Midsummer Night's Dream* explores different aspects of love. Here are some quotations from well-known people to start you thinking about some of these aspects.

Ⓐ *It is good to love in moderate degree, but foolish to love to distraction.*

Plautus

I love thee like a pudding, If I wert pie I'd eat thee.

Proverbial

Ⓑ *It is wrong to think that love comes from long companionship. Love is the offspring of spiritual affinity, and unless that affinity is created in a moment, it will not be created in years or even generations.*

Kahlil Gibran

Love is not love which alters when it alteration finds.

Shakespeare

In married life three is company and two none.

Oscar Wilde

Ⓑ *True love ripens slowly out of friendship; it does not happen suddenly or dramatically.*

Proudhon

Ⓒ *Jealousy is not a barometer by which depth of love can be read; it merely records the degree of the lover's insecurity.*

Margaret Mead

It is not lack of love but lack of friendship that makes unhappy marriages.

Nietzsche

(a) *The lover who is not jealous is not a true lover.*

Capellanus

(A) *When one does not love too much, one does not love enough.*

Pascal

- There are three pairs of quotations here among the ten. In each pair an opposing view of one aspect of love is described. Can you find the pairs?

- Choose one quotation that you think is particularly true or striking, and justify your choice to a partner.

- Look up poems on love in an anthology and discuss with a partner or small group which aspects of love the poems you find are exploring.

2 In *A Midsummer Night's Dream* we see a group of characters leave one setting, the court at Athens, and enter another very different one, the wood outside. The characters' behaviour alters as they move into and out of the wood. Can you think of a place away from your home which brings out different aspects of your character?

In pairs or small groups discuss how your behaviour changes, and what you think are the reasons. You might also discuss how you feel about returning to your home after you have been away.

3 Fairies play an influential role in *A Midsummer Night's Dream*. Discuss the following points in small groups or as a class:

- How did you first hear about fairies as a young child?

- In what different ways have you seen fairies and spirits presented since then?

- What other characters, past or present, from the supernatural world have you come across? These might include figures from films or comics.

- Do these figures tend to present good or evil forces or a mixture of both?

Find out as much as you can about the Elizabethan view of the supernatural and discuss your research as a class. How does it differ from the present-day view?

Following on from your research, you might find it interesting to look at reproductions of paintings inspired by the play. The Tate Gallery in London has a number of these pictures, and sells reproductions by post.

4 Do you think dreams are linked to reality? In pairs or small groups jot down and discuss any thoughts on this subject. Include, where possible, examples of occasions when you have had dreams which have shown you things about yourself.

5 Read the Act summaries of *A Midsummer Night's Dream*. When you are clear about how the plot develops jot down and discuss which episodes you think could be very funny to watch. Explain to a partner why you think they might make you laugh. Think also whether there are any episodes in the play which might make you angry or sad. If there are, which ones might they be and why? (Keep your notes so you can compare your reactions now to when you read or watch a performance of the play itself.)

6 In a small group, choose one of the following situations as the starting point for a discussion or short improvisation. Compare what is covered in your work with other groups that have chosen the same situation.

- A father feels very strongly against the man his daughter wants to go out with. He prefers another man, and forbids her to see the one she likes.

- A girl has been going out with a boy for some time. However, she is now being pursued by her best friend's boyfriend, whom she does not like very much.

- Two couples lost in a wood encounter beings they cannot see but who are able to bewitch them.

- Two friends who are getting married would like a short play put on to entertain them on the evening of their wedding day. What kind of play would be appropriate?

During reading

Act 1

Check your knowledge of Act 1

- What do we learn about Theseus' and Hippolyta's past which differs from the present?
- What is Egeus complaining about to Theseus?
- What decision does Theseus make about Egeus' complaint?
- What is Hermia's reaction to Theseus' decisions?
- What do we learn about Demetrius' past?
- What do Hermia and Lysander decide to do in response to Theseus' ruling?
- What does Helena decide to do when Hermia and Lysander tell her about their plan?
- Why have the workmen assembled together?
- How does Bottom show his enthusiasm for acting?

Questioning the text in Act 1

1. What is your impression of Hippolyta and Theseus' relationship? Discuss your thoughts in small groups, remembering to back up your opinions with evidence from the text.

2. In the argument over Hermia's marriage in scene 1, do you sympathise with one character more than the others? If so, why?

3.   But Demetrius, come;
   And come Egeus, you shall go with me;
   I have some private schooling for you both.
                         (lines 114–16)

   What does Theseus mean by 'private schooling'? Role play or write down what happens at this meeting.

4 Imagine that Theseus and Hippolyta discuss the difficulties between Egeus and Hermia after they have left. Role play or write down their conversation.

5 After the events of this day, each of the four young lovers writes a diary. Choose two, and write their entries.

6 How would you describe Bottom? Find evidence from the text for each descriptive word you use.

Can you think of a modern-day personality who is similar? If so, what is it about this person that she or he has in common with Bottom?

7 Imagine Peter Quince returns home and talks to his wife about the first meeting of his theatre group. How would he describe it? Role play or write down their conversation.

8 You are about to move into a very different setting and atmosphere in the next act. Before reading on, make clear to yourself what sort of place the court is under Theseus' rule.

Here is a list of adjectives. In pairs, choose five which you feel describe the court best. Then, on your own, find examples from the text to back up your choices, and see if they are the same ones as your partner has used.

reasonable	ordered	pompous
democratic	unkind	unemotional
tyrannical	calm	ruled by law
male dominated	formal	civilised

9 Look back at the scene and check where Shakespeare has used rhymed verse, unrhymed verse and prose. Can you explain why he changed where he did?

Act 2

Check your knowledge of Act 2

- Why, according to Puck, is Oberon angry?
- In what way has Oberon shown his anger and jealousy?
- What is Demetrius' attitude towards Helena when we first meet them in the wood?
- What does Oberon ask Puck to do with the juice he has just collected? What is Oberon himself going to do with it?
- What picture of the wood do the fairies build up with their lullaby?
- When Oberon puts the juice onto Titania's eyelids, what does he hope will be there for her to see when she wakes?
- About what do Hermia and Lysander disagree before they sleep?
- What mistake does Puck make with the juice, and what result does this have?

Questioning the text in Act 2

1. Eight different characters involved in love relationships have now been introduced and, with them, different aspects of behaviour in love. Using a table with three columns like the one below, headed *Theseus and Hippolyta, Oberon and Titania* and *The Young Lovers*, try to establish as many differences in their relationships as you can. Work in pairs or small groups, and then compare your findings with others. Add to these columns as you read the rest of the play.

Theseus and Hippolyta	Oberon and Titania	The Young Lovers
conquering – Theseus wins Hippolyta in battle	passionate and jealous relationships	naive, innocent

2. The young lovers would certainly not have seen their experiences in this act as funny. So what is it about the scenes that makes us laugh? Think about the situations, the language and the actions of the characters as they might be directed in performance.

With a partner, choose a short extract from one of the following episodes so that you can prove your case for what creates the humour, with specific as well as general examples.

check

- Act 2, scene 1, lines 188–244
- Act 2, scene 2, lines 34–64
- Act 2, scene 2, lines 83–155

3 In Acts 1 and 2, we have seen Theseus, Oberon and Titania each ruling over different groups. How would you compare and contrast them as leaders so far? Discuss in pairs or small groups and report back to the class.

4 Which of the following adjectives would you use to describe the wood and the world of the fairies? Copy the list out, put a tick or cross by each one and then compare your results with those of a partner. Challenge them to back up at least five of their words with evidence from the text.

lawless	chaotic	dangerous	erotic
disorganised	organised	good	cruel
evil	magical	exotic	haunted
violent	beautiful	calm	exciting
wild	emotional	lush	nocturnal

5 Go through Act 2 and find all the references that are made to animals. Why do you think Shakespeare uses so much animal imagery in this act?

6 In this act, Shakespeare creates a number of pictures of the natural world in words. For instance, at the beginning of the act, a fairy describes cowslips like this:

> The cowslips tall her pensioners be;
> In their gold coats spots you see,
> Those be rubies, fairy favours,
> In those freckles live their savours.
> I must go seek some dew-drops here,
> And hang a pearl in every cowslip's ear.

(lines 10–15)

Which pictures remain in your head now? Describe them briefly in y our own words to a partner and see if they recognise which part of the text your pictures come from.

Finally, go through both scenes listing some of the places where Shakespeare seems to be creating a detailed picture in words which you can clearly visualise. Choose one of these scenes to illustrate, remembering to include all the details in the text.

Act 3

Check your knowledge of Act 3

- Remind yourself of which parts in 'Pyramus and Thisby' each of the workmen are to play?
- The workmen find a number of problems in putting on the play. What are these difficulties, how are they resolved, and who resolves them?
- What happens to Bottom just after the rehearsal has started? What are his friends' reactions to this?
- How does Titania order her attendants to treat Bottom?
- When Oberon realises Puck's mistake, what does he do first? What situation does this result in between the lovers?
- What is Puck's attitude to the humans and the confusion they are in?
- Why do Hermia and Helena argue?
- What are Oberon's next instructions to Puck before Lysander and Demetrius re-enter? When does Puck carry out his orders?

Questioning the text in Act 3

1 Which parts of the rehearsal of 'Pyramus and Thisby' did you find funny? See if a partner had the same response. Discuss together how Shakespeare created the humour in these parts.

2 In the episode where Bottom is left on his own, and Titania wakes up and falls in love with him (scene 1, lines 118–158), much of the humour is

created by words having more meaning than their speaker realises. This is called dramatic irony. With a partner, list each occasion when this device is used, then try to find other examples from earlier in the play.

3 In scene 2, lines 64–73, animal imagery is used by the lovers. Think back to assignment 5 of 'Questioning the text in Act 2' on page 218 and discuss whether Shakespeare is aiming for the same effect here. Try to find other examples of animal images used as the scene progresses and see if the effect is the same.

4 List the insults that Hermia and Helena level at one another in scene 2, lines 282–325. Can you make up some particularly rich insults to hurl at a partner (who is also a friend!)?

5 Do you feel sorry for any of the characters in scene 2 of this act? If so when and why? Compare your thoughts with those of a partner.

6 Imagine Puck was retelling the mischief he has created to a friend later. What would he say? Either role-play or write down his speech.

Act 4

Check your knowledge of Act 4

- How is Bottom behaving in the opening scene?
- Why does Oberon release Titania from the spell?
- Oberon tells us that 'tomorrow midnight' the lovers will marry. How accurately has Shakespeare handled the timing of the play?
- If you were producing this play what tone of voice would you give to Theseus and Hippolyta's comparison of the sound of their hounds?
- How does Theseus respond to Egeus' objections to the lovers' new situation?
- How do the lovers react to what has happened?
- What is Bottom's reaction when he reflects on his time as an ass?

- What happens when Bottom meets the other workmen again?
- In this act, order is gradually restored after a period of chaos. Go through the scene and identify each area of confusion and its solution.

Questioning the text in Act 4

1 Read Oberon's speech in scene 1, lines 47–64. With a partner, improvise the conversation described.

Now imagine that Titania tells Bottom about her meeting with Oberon, and improvise this scene as well. (This conversation would have occurred just before the opening of Act 4.)

Having done this, have you formed any views about why Titania's behaviour towards Oberon, as described in his speech, seems so different from her attitude to him earlier in the play?

2 Titania's behaviour to Oberon after he has released her from his spell remains a contrast to her behaviour towards him in Act 2. Are there any questions or points you would like to put to Titania or Oberon about their relationship now? Write these in the form of a letter and then write the answer they might have sent you.

Act 5

Check your knowledge of Act 5

- To what does Theseus compare lovers in his long opening speech, and for what reasons?
- What is Hippolyta's reaction to his claim?
- Is Philostrate's description of the play that Bottom and the workmen are to perform a fair one?
- Why does Theseus want to see the play? What is his attitude to the players?
- What are Demetrius' and Lysander's reactions to the play?
- In what sort of language do the actors in 'Pyramus and Thisby' speak? What

effect does this have on the picture of love we are presented with?

- Do Theseus' and Hippolyta's reactions to the play differ, and if so, how?

- Sum up the story of 'Pyramus and Thisby'. Does it have anything in common with the story of the four young lovers in *A Midsummer Night's Dream*?

- What have the fairies come to do when they enter the house at the end?

- To what 'visions' is Puck referring in his final speech? What is he asking the audience to do?

Questioning the text in Act 5

1. In Theseus's opening speech he talks about the similarities between lunatics, lovers and poets. With a partner, draw up a table of what the two of you think are the similarities and differences between them.

   Re-read his speech carefully (scene 1, lines 2–22) and discuss how far you agree or disagree with him. What do you think of Hippolyta's reply to Theseus (lines 23–7)?

2. Here are some statements about 'Pyramus and Thisby'. Discuss them with a partner or in a small group and decide which ones you agree with, and which you disagree with.

   - 'Pyramus and Thisby' is merely a bit of light relief at the end of the play.

   - The performance of 'Pyramus and Thisby' is a good way of getting all the humans together on stage for the last act of the play.

   - The actors in 'Pyramus and Thisby' are taking their jobs seriously and doing their best.

   - There are similarities between the situation of Pyramus and Thisby and that of Lysander and Hermia in Act 1.

   - The inflated language used in 'Pyramus and Thisby' is nothing like the language used by the lovers to express their passion.

   - The reaction of the nobles to the play is coarse and insensitive.

- The young lovers (or at least Demetrius and Lysander) fail to see the connection between their recent behaviour and that of the lovers in 'Pyramus and Thisby'.
- 'Pyramus and Thisby' is not suitable for a wedding celebration.
- Theseus and Hippolyta react to the play in different ways.

3 Sometimes the reappearance of Oberon, Titania, Puck and the other fairies in lines 360–411 is cut from performances. Here are some reasons for keeping them in. Put them into your order of importance.

- Puck has been a popular character, so the audience will want to see him again at the end.
- The fairies are creatures of the night, so it is appropriate to bring them back at this point.
- We need to see that Oberon and Titania are properly reconciled to one another.
- The words of the court and the wood need to be unified, because they have presented two different types of attitude and behaviour. Each is needed to modify the other.
- A song and dance rounds off an entertaining play well.
- We need reminding that the happiness of the humans has been brought about by the fairies.

After reading

Plot

1 Write a series of true and false statements about the situations in the play. Test a partner on which is which.

For example:

Egeus favours Lysander, not Demetrius .	False
Hippolyta and Theseus have fought in the past!	True

223

2 In a group, choose moments from the play which seemed to you to be particularly funny as you read it. Produce these as silent tableaux. See if other groups can work out which moment is being presented, and which character is which.

3 A journalist working on the gossip column of *The Athens Times* has been talking to Philostrate who has heard something of what went on in the wood. Think about what conversations Philostrate might have overheard and what he might have been told or what assumptions he might have made.

Role-play the dialogue between the journalist and Philostrate, and then write up the newspaper article.

4 What sort of headlines would different types of newspapers use if they had discovered what had gone on in the woods that night? Look at a range of newspapers to remind yourself of how headlines vary among them and what techniques are used to attract the readers' attention.

Now imagine two journalists, one from a 'serious' broadsheet, the other from the popular tabloid press, each covering the story for their papers. Decide what their sources would be, who they would have interviewed, etc. Role-play their interviews, and then write up the articles. Before you do this, discuss carefully how the papers' presentation of the stories would differ.

Character

1 Look at the cast list and decide which are major characters and which minor, and why.

2 Identify the speaker in the following quotations. Then check the text to see if you've got them right:

> If thou lov'st me, then,
> Steal forth thy father's house tomorrow night;
>
> (Act 1, scene 1, lines 163–4)

Lord, what fools these mortals be!

(Act 3, scene 2, line 115)

No, no, you must play Pyramus, and Flute, you Thisby.

(Act 1, scene 2, lines 51–2)

Love, therefore, and tongue-tied simplicity,
In least speak most, to my capacity.

(Act 5, scene 1, lines 104–5)

How came these things to pass?
O, how mine eyes do loathe his visage now!

(Act 4, scene 1, lines 79–80)

And all the faith, the virtue of my heart,
The object and the pleasure of mine eye,
Is only Helena.

(Act 4, scene 1, lines 170–2)

And I am such a tender ass, if my hair do but tickle me, I must scratch.

(Act 4, scene 1, lines 26–7)

O me! you juggler, you canker-blossom,
You thief of love! What, have you come by night
And stolen my love's heart from him?

(Act 3, scene 2, lines 282–4)

Tarry, rash wanton; am not I thy lord?

(Act 2, scene 1, line 63)

Use me but as your spaniel; spurn me, strike me,

(Act 2, scene 1, line 205)

I love not to see wretchedness o'ercharged,
And duty in his service perishing.

(Act 5, scene 1, lines 85–6)

3 In pairs or small groups, collect as many words as you can to describe a chosen character. For each word, find a quotation or a piece of action from the play to back up your choice. Point out any words which could apply to more than one character because of their similar attitudes and actions.

225

Share your words with other pairs or groups. Challenge each other if the words do not seem appropriate.

4. Individually or with a partner, imagine a chosen character as things other than a person. If this character were a piece of furniture, weather, a musical instrument, an animal or a car, think about what sort of furniture, weather, instrument, animal or car they would be. If Puck were a car, for instance, perhaps he would be a Mini with a particularly powerful engine, and if Bottom were a type of weather, he might be a sunny day. Compare your results with other people in your class.

5. Write horoscopes for Oberon, Titania, Puck, Bottom or one of the young lovers the day before the night in the wood.

6. Write a letter from one of the characters to an actor about to play their part in a production. The character would need to explain in detail what they are like, and how to make them appear in particular scenes.

7. At the end of the play, the humans involved in the events in the wood are only just beginning to reflect on what has happened. Imagine you are one of them, sifting through what happened in the wood a week, a year or ten years later. In pairs, act out what you think would be said. (It may help to write brief notes first.) Write this up as a dialogue or as a letter to a friend.

   Alternatively, write this reflection in the form of a diary entry or a television interview. (If you completed assignment 5 in 'Questioning the text in Act 1 on page 216, your answer may help you here.)

8. Write two short reviews of 'The most lamentable comedy and most cruel death of Pyramus and Thisby', one for *The Athenian Workers' News* which is a paper read by Bottom and his friends and one for *The Courtier* which is read by the nobles.

9. Learn a speech or a part of a speech spoken by your favourite character. Begin by reading it through, making sure from the glossary that you know exactly what it means, and reminding yourself of where it occurs in the

overall story of the play. Think about what mood the character is in at this point and what they might be feeling. This will help you to decide what kind of voice you should use. Think also about what actions the character might be making as they speak the lines.

Act the lines before a group, explaining beforehand how your passage fits into the play and why you have chosen it.

Themes

1️⃣ Below is a list of statements which describe key ideas in the play. Place them in what you consider to be their order of importance. Compare your order with a partner's and back up your decisions where they differ.

The play is about:

- the way the upper classes treat the lower classes;
- the right to choose your own partner in marriage;
- calm and reason as opposed to passion and instinct;
- the irrational way people behave when in love;
- the way love makes us behave cruelly to people;
- the power of the supernatural world;
- the meaningfulness of dreams;
- the way we use our imaginations when watching plays;
- how simplicity and good humour can triumph over difficulties;
- the tension between men and women in love relationships.

2️⃣ Look at the following quotations. Which would you choose to illustrate the statements listed in the previous assignment? You may find it useful to look at the context in which the words are spoken in the scene.

> DEMETRIUS
> Tempt not too much the hatred of my spirit;
> For I am sick when I do look on thee.

(Act 2, scene 1, 211–2)

THESEUS

> The best in this kind are but shadows, and the worst are no worse, if
> imagination amend them.

> > (Act 5, scene 1, lines 207–8)

HELENA

> If you were men, as men you are in show,
> You would not use a gentle lady so;

> > (Act 3, scene 2, lines 151–2)

EGEUS

> I beg the ancient privilege of Athens;
> As she is mine, I may dispose of her;

> > (Act 1, scene 1, lines 41–2)

BOTTOM

> ... and yet, to say the truth, reason and love keep little company together
> nowadays.

> > (Act 3, scene 1, lines 141–2)

THESEUS

> Our sport shall be to take what they mistake;

> > (Act 5, scene 1, line 90)

TITANIA

> > The spring, the summer,
> The childing autumn, angry winter, change
> Their wonted liveries, and the mazéd world,
> By their increase, now knows not which is which.
> And this same progeny of evils comes
> From our debate, from our dissension;
> We are their parents and original.

> > (Act 2, scene 1, lines 111–7)

BOTTOM

> The eye of man hath not heard, the ear of man hath not seen, man's hand
> is not able to taste, his tongue to conceive, nor his heart to report, what my
> dream was. I will get Peter Quince to write a ballad of this dream; it shall
> be called 'Bottom's Dream', because it hath no bottom; and I will sing it in
> the latter end of a play, before the Duke.

> > (Act 4, scene 1, lines 212–8)

THESEUS

    Lovers and madmen have such seething brains,
    Such shaping fantasies, that apprehend
    More than cool reason ever comprehends.

                          (Act 5, scene 1, lines 4–6)

HIPPOLYTA

    And all their minds transfigured so together,
    More witnesseth than fancy's images,
    And grows to something of great constancy;
    But howsoever, strange and admirable.

                        (Act 5, scene 1, lines 24–7)

- With a partner or in a small group look again at the statements in Assignment 1 and choose *three* which you think are particularly important. Find your own examples from the play that illustrate especially well the three themes you have chosen.

- Use the information you have gathered to hold a class debate on which are the major themes of the play.

- Follow up this work by writing a short talk outlining the relevance of the play's themes to modern life. It should be aimed at convincing a reluctant audience who are not familiar with the plays of Shakespeare.

3 You may already have considered the exploration of different aspects of love in previous tasks before and during your reading of the play. Below is a list of adjectives which describe some views of love in *A Midsummer Night's Dream* as a whole. In pairs or small groups, find examples from the play for each adjective. Can you add a final adjective?

irrational	inconsistent	obsessive	comic
jealous	rational	defiant	harmonious
unselfish	confusing	cruel	?

Which of the four couples who are together at the end of the play do you think has the best chance of lasting happiness? Why?

4 EITHER

Imagine that the love lives of Hermia, Helena, Hippolyta and Titania are the subject of a feature in a magazine. The article would include the writer's comparisons of their relationships and the characters' own thoughts on their recent experiences of love.

OR

Write an essay on the different aspects of love in *A Midsummer Night's Dream*.

5 The human characters in *A Midsummer Night's Dream* change their behaviour depending on where they are, and whether it is day or night. In order to explore this aspect of the play, divide a piece of paper into four, and label the four sections 'Athens: day', 'the wood: night', 'the wood: day' and 'Athens: night'. Divide up the action of the play into the four sections.

Imagine that a reincarnated Shakespeare is writing a letter to the director of a new film version of the play. He wants to stress the importance of the two settings and times. What would he write to explain this aspect in detail? Remember to make close reference to the play. (If you have completed them, your answers to 'Questioning the text in Act 1' assignment 8 on page 216 and 'in Act 2' assignment 4 on page 218 will help.)

6 Before reading the play you might have discussed different images of fairies and completed assignment 3 in the 'Themes' section on page 213. Now you have direct experience of the play, you should be familiar with Shakespeare's fairies, and will have gathered that these are rather different from the fairy godmother in Cinderella or the fairy on top of your Christmas tree!

In pairs or small groups make a class wall display illustrating the conclusions you have come to about the fairies in the play. This could include the following:

- brief character studies of Oberon, Titania and Puck;
- quotations from the play which illustrate the fairies' natures;
- key adjectives which describe the fairies;

- costume designs. You may have several alternatives for each of the characters. Look through the photographs in the book to see what costumes have been used in some recent productions;
- set designs for the wood the fairies inhabit. Refer back to the text to give you ideas. Act 2, scene 1, lines 249–56; Act 2, scene 2, lines 9–23; and Act 3, scene 1, lines 163–71 should help you.

Make your display as visually striking and varied as you can.

7 In Act 4, scene 1, when dawn breaks and the sleeping mortals in the wood wake up, they cannot believe that what they experienced during the night was real:

DEMETRIUS

> Are you sure
> That we are awake? It seems to me
> That yet we sleep, we dream. (lines 193–5)

BOTTOM

> I have had a dream past the wit of man to say what dream it was.
> (lines 206–7)

At the end of the play, Puck compares what the audience has just seen to a dream:

PUCK

> If we shadows have offended,
> Think but this, and all is mended,
> That you have but slumbered here,
> While these visions did appear.
> And this weak and idle theme,
> No more yielding than a dream,
> Gentles do not reprehend:

(Act 5, scene 1, lines 412–8)

Using your own knowledge of dreams, discuss in small groups:

- what it was about the experiences of the lovers and Bottom in the wood that was dream-like;

231

- the similarities between the experience of watching a play in the theatre and dreaming.

Record your discussion on tape. Exchange recordings with other groups, and throw open the discussion to the class as a whole.

8 In a small group, discuss which comedy programmes you have seen and enjoyed on television. Make a list of the kind of humour each one displays: it may be in the language, such as jokes which depend on wordplay or the description of a funny situation; in the situation itself, where, for example, one character may have lost control of events or does not know something that is known by the audience; it may be visual, when appearances and actions make you laugh. Can you think of other categories of humour of your own?

- Identify which parts of *A Midsummer Night's Dream* you found funniest. Decide which type, or types, of humour Shakespeare has created in these parts.
- Using the information you have now collected, write an essay on how the comedy is created in *A Midsummer Night's Dream*.

In performance

1 Sometimes productions of *A Midsummer Night's Dream* are given with some of the text cut. This may be because of time restrictions, or the limited memories of amateur actors in learning their lines!

Imagine that you are directing a new production and *have* to cut about ten to twenty per cent of the play. Organise yourselves into groups of five, and in each group, allocate one person to each act. Decide which lines in your act you will cut. Remember that the play still has to make perfect sense to the audience. When you have finished, discuss what you have done with the other four people in your group and see if you agree.

Now form a new group of all the people from the other groups in the class who were working on your act, and compare your cuts with theirs.

2 Over the last twenty years or so productions of *A Midsummer Night's Dream* have varied greatly in the kind of costumes that have been used. Some have been in Elizabethan costumes, some in modern dress, and some in costumes from no specific time or place. In a small group, discuss the advantages and disadvantages of these approaches.

Now imagine that you have been given the job of costume designer for a new production of the play which will be in modern dress. Design costumes for the following characters:

- Theseus in Act 1;
- Hermia in the wood;
- Bottom in the wood;
- Titania;
- Puck.

3 You are the casting director of a new production of the play. Look through some magazines for pictures of people who you think would be suitable for some of the parts in the play. Try to find suitable faces for at least Bottom, Puck, Oberon, Titania, Theseus and one pair of the young lovers. Alternatively, you could draw your idea of the characters. Mount the pictures and add brief notes on the character to help the actor.

4 Some productions have the same actors playing the parts of Theseus and Oberon, Hippolyta and Titania, or Philostrate and Puck. In pairs discuss why you think this is done. Do you think this is a good idea?

5 All we are told about the location of Acts 2 to 4 is that it is 'A wood near Athens'. Some designers use a detailed and realistic set while others use simply a bare stage and lighting effects.

Take on the role of the designer of the set for this section of the play. Draw a plan of the stage, showing where various things happen, and draw a picture of what the stage would look like from the audience's viewpoint.

6 In small groups, choose an important scene or episode from the play, and prepare a workshop performance of it to be presented to the rest of the

class. Set, props and costume should be extremely simple or non-existent. The words should, if possible, be memorised.

After the performances, discuss why each group chose their scene and which performance came closest to capturing the atmosphere of the play.

7 Write a review of a production of *A Midsummer Night's Dream* you have seen either at the theatre or on video.

In your review you will need to tell your readers something about your understanding of the play's themes and characters, and your judgement of how well the production reflected them. You will also need to comment on the set, casting, use of lighting and music and so on:

Language

1 Three of the threads of imagery that run through the play are: the moon, eyes and seeing, and animals.

- Divide yourselves into three groups, so that each group can research one of these threads:

a) The play starts with a conversation about the moon, contains many references to the moon, and even has a character playing the part of the moon!

Find as many references to the moon as you can from the play, using the glossary to help you work out the significance of each. In each case try to work out what function this reference has, and whether it connects to the way images of the moon are being used elsewhere.

b) In Acts 2 and 3 in the wood, animal imagery is often used by the lovers and the fairies. If you have not already collected these references in 'Questioning the text in Act 2', assignment 5 on page 218 and 'in Act 3', assignment 3 on page 220, do so now.

Look at how some of this animal imagery recurs in the last scene of the play and in the performance of 'Pyramus and Thisby'. Discuss what reasons Shakespeare may have had for reintroducing it.

c) Shakespeare makes many references in the play to eyes and sight to show the way the people in love think that they see the truth but are often blinded by love ... or a magic spell.

Find these references and discuss in each case whether the character speaking is really seeing clearly or not.

- At the end of your research your group's conclusions should be written down so that you can present your findings to the others in a spoken presentation. Alternatively, you can make a tape recording for exchange between groups.

- After you have completed all the above, write an essay on Shakespeare's use of imagery in the play.

2 The play uses the following types of language:

- rhymed verse in ten-syllable lines
- unrhymed verse in ten-syllable lines
- rhymed verse in seven-syllable lines
- rhymed verse with varying line-lengths
- songs
- prose

In groups, try to decide which kinds of language are used by the following groups of characters. (They may use more than one type.)

- Theseus, Hippolyta, Egeus and Philostrate
- Hermia, Helena, Lysander and Demetrius
- Bottom and the other workmen
- characters in 'Pyramus and Thisby'
- fairies

When you have reached conclusions, compare your findings with those of other groups. Go on to discuss Shakespeare's reasons for varying the type of language in the play.

3   Reread the following extracts from speeches by Oberon and Titania in Act 2, scene 1:

- lines 88–100
- lines 123–34
- lines 155–68

These are all pictures in words. Choose one of them, and turn it into modern English using the glossary. Try to end with a version that still contains all the sense, and is understandable without notes. You may also wish to produce an illustration. This should show close attention to all the details.

Read through the two versions, and decide what has been lost in your 'translation'. Think carefully about the sound, rhythm and choice of words.

Further assignments

1   Imagine that the workmen decide to put on a play called 'Bottom's Dream' based on Bottom's adventures in the wood. Write a scene from this play which a group of you then act out.

2   Imagine you are competing alongside Bottom and his friends to produce something that would be appropriate for Theseus and Hippolyta's wedding celebrations. Write a short play, poem or song that you feel would be suitable for this purpose.

3   Imagine that you have been commissioned to design a programme for a forthcoming production of *A Midsummer Night's Dream*. It will need to provide information about the play and the actors at the same time as being visually appealing. Prepare this programme using the list below to help you plan its contents:

- cover design
- very brief plot summary
- some reflections on the themes of the play
- photos of the actors taking the central roles

- photos of this production.

Try to find copies of programmes from past productions of *A Midsummer Night's Dream* and other plays, especially by The Royal Shakespeare Company, to inspire you.

4   Music is introduced on several occasions in *A Midsummer Night's Dream*. Identify where these places are and what purpose the music serves.

Listen to the overture that Mendelssohn wrote for the play and discuss how effectively he has captured the feelings and atmosphere of the different parts. You might find it interesting to compare it to extracts taken from Benjamin Britten's full-length opera based on the play. Written in 1960, it is quite difficult to listen to but it is also very atmospheric.

See if you can find other pieces of music, classical or modern, which you think would suit certain characters or moments in the play.

5   *As You Like It* is another Shakespearean comedy that makes use of contrasting court and forest settings. Read the play and find as many general points of comparison and contrast as you can.

6   *Love's Labour's Lost*, a comedy written by Shakespeare a few years before *A Midsummer Night's Dream*, also concerns the ups and downs of young lovers. It too concludes with a performance put on by lower-status characters to entertain the nobility.

Read Act 5 of *Love's Labour's Lost* and write an essay comparing and contrasting it to Act 5 of *A Midsummer Night's Dream*. Consider the following:

- the sort of language used by the noble characters;
- the sort of language used in the 'play within the play';
- the treatment given to the performers by the nobles;
- the difference in tone and feeling between the rather melancholy end of *Love's Labour's Lost* and the more celebratory end of *A Midsummer Night's Dream*.

Study questions

Many of the activities you have already completed (pages 211–36: before, during and after reading the play) will help you to answer the following questions. Before you begin to write, consider these points about essay writing:

- Spend some time deciding exactly what the essay question is asking. It may be useful to break the sentence down into phrases or words and decide what each part means.

- Focusing on the areas you have decided are relevant, note down as many quotations or references to the play as you can think of which are relevant to the answer.

- Decide on a shape which you think will be appropriate for the essay. It may be useful to think of a literal shape which will suit the argument.

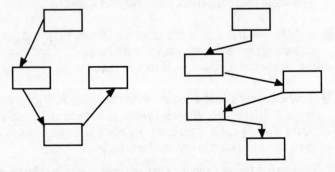

- Organise your ideas and quotations into sections to fit your shape; you could do this by placing notes into different piles.

- Write a first draft of your essay.

- Redraft as many times as you need to, taking care to consider the following:
  Does this answer the question?
  Is this essay easy to read, with clear organisation in which one point flows on to another?

Do the opening and concluding paragraphs seem clear and linked to the question set?

Are there any spelling or grammatical errors? Use a dictionary and thesaurus.

1 'The course of true love never did run smooth.' How far does the presentation of characters in love in *A Midsummer Night's Dream* confirm this statement?

2 'Lovers and madmen have such seething brains.' Discuss the way in which love is seen as a form of madness in *A Midsummer Night's Dream*.

3 It is thought that *A Midsummer Night's Dream* was written to celebrate a wedding. How suitable do you think it would be for this purpose?

4 Discuss the ways in which 'The most lamentable comedy and most cruel death of Pyramus and Thisby' is related to the main play.

5 One of the fascinating aspects of the play is the way in which the stories of three independent groups – the lovers, the workmen and the fairies – are separate yet intertwined. Discuss the way in which the various plots in *A Midsummer Night's Dream* are linked together.

6 'Lord what fools these mortals be!' To what extent do you think that Puck is justified in his comment?

7 'The nobles may see themselves as superior to the workmen but they are deluded.' To what extent do you agree with this statement?

8 Discuss the relationship between:

- Hermia and Helena,
- Oberon and Puck.

9. Demetrius describes himself as 'wood within this wood'. Discuss how far this description could apply to the other humans when the enter the wood.

10. Discuss the contrasts between the court of Athens and the wood outside. Include in your answer your thoughts about why Shakespeare used two such different environments.

11. 'The humour in *A Midsummer Night's Dream* comes as much from the language as the situations.' Discuss these two sources of comedy with close reference to the play.

12. *A Midsummer Night's Dream* is seen as a comedy. However there are elements in the play which threaten the overall happy effect. Which episodes seemed to you to contain less happy aspects? Include in your answer how these are not allowed to unbalance the play as a comedy.

13. 'Humour helps us face up to our frailty.' Discuss this statement with reference to *A Midsummer Night's Dream*.

14. What contribution does magic make to *A Midsummer Night's Dream*?

15. Discuss the way in which Shakespeare has used dreams in *A Midsummer Night's Dream*.

16. 'One of the great delights of *A Midsummer Night's Dream* is the richness and variety of its language.' Discuss this claim with close reference to the text.

17. Choose any three relationships or characters in the play which seem to you to provide good grounds for comparison and contrast.

18. Choose a scene which made a particular impression on you and show, by close reference to the text, where its impact lay. In your answer you need to consider aspects such as characters, action, setting, language and atmosphere.

Using part of the text

Below are two suggestions for using just a part of the text of *A Midsummer Night's Dream*. You do not need to have read or seen the whole play in order to complete them.

▓ The Workmen's Play

Act 5, scene 1 of the play is one of the funniest parts of *A Midsummer Night's Dream*. Some workmen from Athens have prepared a play to show to the king and queen in court. They are not very good actors and they make several mistakes which the nobles, and the audience, find funny.

- In a group of twelve read through the scene with eleven of you reading the parts and the twelfth reading the stage instructions.

- On a large piece of paper work as a group to decide where each person might stand in the scene, how the court is laid out, and what the stage will look like. Having done this, position yourselves in order to act out the scene. The twelfth person now becomes the director. Act through the scene once.

- On your second run-through you should know, in general terms, what is said so you could ad-lib the scene, or even learn some of the words by heart. The characters or the director could add in some additional actions for characters: in some productions the nobles erupt into fits of giggles; one of the workmen could have stage fright or could keep forgetting his lines and need prompting.

- Now return to your planning page and decide what costumes you want your characters to wear. You could get together these costumes and even have a go at making some props or items for the set to match your production.

- In your next run-through act your scene out to an audience and get the director to notice which parts of the scene the audience finds especially funny. In a final run-through, parts which did not work can be cut and additional funny pieces added in.

- Make a suitable programme for your performance to give to the audience.

241

You could also look at some comic scenes from other plays by Shakespeare and carry out the same tasks with them. Here are some to look out for:

Act 2, scene 5 of *Twelfth Night* where a mischievous servant sets a trap to make another servant look foolish.

Act 2, scene 1 of *The Taming of the Shrew* where Petruchio tries to woo Katherine.

Act 2, scene 2 of *The Tempest* where a drunken Stephano finds his friend Trinculo.

2 A Jealous Argument

Titania and Oberon are king and queen of the fairies who live and rule in a magical wood near Athens. In Act 2, scene 1 of the play they fight over a young Indian prince whom Titania has and Oberon wants. Before they enter we hear about the argument from one of Titania's fairies and Oberon's servant, Puck. When Oberon and Titania meet it is night time and we hear how their argument has upset the natural order in nature.

- Read through Act 2, scene 1, lines 1–145.

- Working in pairs, draw some sketches of Oberon, Titania, Puck and the fairies, remembering that they are not human and need to look like spirits. Remember that the actors playing them would be people wearing costumes and make-up.

- Now sketch an illustration of the setting of the wood lit by moonlight.

- Using these sketches as a basis, draw up a cartoon story-board of the scene, including at least some of the words spoken and as many of the actions as you can identify.

Shakespeare includes spirits and enchanted places in many of his other plays. You could complete the same tasks as noted above on a scene from one such play. You might like to look at:

Act 1, scenes 1 and 2 of *The Tempest* in which Prospero, a human with the ability to use magic, creates a sea storm through his servant spirit Ariel.

Act 1, scenes 1 and 3; Act 3, scene 5; and Act 4, scene 1 of *Macbeth* in which three witches meet together in order to carry out evil deeds.

Longman Group UK Limited,
Longman House, Burnt Mill, Harlow,
Essex CM20 2JE, England
and Associated Companies throughout the world.

© Longman Group UK Limited 1992

First published 1992
Second impression 1992

Editorial material set in 10/12 point Helvetica Light Condensed
Produced by Longman Singapore (Pte) Ltd
Printed in Singapore

ISBN 0 582 08833 X

Cover illustration by Reg Cartwright

The Publisher's policy is to use paper manufactured from sustainable forests.

Longman Literature
Series editor: Roy Blatchford

Novels

Jane Austen *Pride and Prejudice* 0 582 07720 6
Charlotte Brontë *Jane Eyre* 0 582 07719 2
Emily Brontë *Wuthering Heights* 0 582 07782 6
Charles Dickens *Great Expectations* 0 582 07783 4
F Scott Fitzgerald *The Great Gatsby* 0 582 06023 0
Nadine Gordimer *July's People* 0 582 06011 7
Graham Greene *The Captain and the Enemy* 0 582 06024 9
Thomas Hardy *Far from the Madding Crowd* 0 582 07788 5
Aldous Huxley *Brave New World* 0 582 06016 8
Robin Jenkins *The Cone-Gatherers* 0 582 06017 6
Doris Lessing *The Fifth Child* 0 582 06021 4
Joan Lindsay *Picnic at Hanging Rock* 0 582 08174 2
Bernard Mac Laverty *Lamb* 0 582 06557 7
Brian Moore *Lies of Silence* 0 582 08170 X
George Orwell *Animal Farm* 0 582 06010 9
 Nineteen Eighty-Four 0 582 06018 4
Alan Paton *Cry, The Beloved Country* 0 582 07787 7
Paul Scott *Staying On* 0 582 07718 4

Plays

Alan Ayckbourn *Absurd Person Singular* 0 582 06020 6
J B Priestley *An Inspector Calls* 0 582 06012 5
Terence Rattigan *The Winslow Boy* 0 582 06019 2
Willy Russell *Educating Rita* 0 582 06013 3
 Shirley Valentine 0 582 08173 4
Peter Shaffer *The Royal Hunt of the Sun* 0 582 06014 1
Bernard Shaw *Arms and the Man* 0 582 07785 0
 Pygmalion 0 582 06015 X
 Saint Joan 0 582 07786 9
Oscar Wilde *The Importance of Being Earnest* 0 582 07784 2

Short stories

Jeffrey Archer *A Twist in the Tale* 0 582 06022 2
Bernard Mac Laverty *The Mac Laverty Collection* 0 582 08172 6